IF IT'S BROKE, FIX IT *FAST!*

This book is about broken windows in business—how they happen, why they happen, why they are ignored, and the fatal consequences that can result from their being allowed to go unchecked . . . Even if you don't think that little things make a difference, this book may save your business. If you don't run a business but would like to, this can be the roadmap to your success.

BROKEN WINDOWS, BROKEN BUSINESS
As Featured in *Harvard Business Review*

"With this great book, Michael Levine offers a whole new way to fix things: by starting with the things that are easiest to fix."
> —Larry Winget, bestselling author of
> *Shut Up, Stop Whining, and Get a Life*

"Brisk and well-written...plenty of smart tactical advice."
> —*Psychology Today*

"The major point is a good one: When it comes to problems, 'nothing is small and absolutely nothing is insignificant.'"
> —*New York Times*

"The examples ring true and the fundamentals apply to any size business."
> —*Booklist*

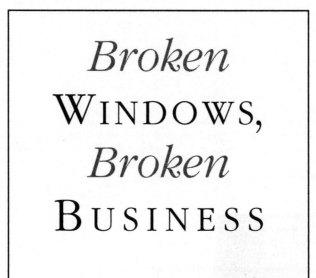

Broken WINDOWS, *Broken* BUSINESS

How the Smallest Remedies Reap the Biggest Rewards

MICHAEL LEVINE

BUSINESS PLUS

NEW YORK   BOSTON

Business Plus
Hachette Book Group
237 Park Avenue
New York, NY 10017

Visit our website at www.HachetteBookGroup.com.

Printed in the United States of America

Originally published in hardcover by Hachette Book Group.

First Trade Edition: November 2006
10 9 8 7 6 5 4 3

Business Plus is an imprint of Grand Central Publishing.
The Business Plus name and logo are trademarks of Hachette Book Group, Inc.

The Library of Congress has cataloged the hardcover edition as follows:

Levine, Michael
    Broken windows, broken business : how the smallest remedies reap the biggest rewards / Michael Levine.— 1st ed.
        p. cm.
    Includes index.
    ISBN 978-0-446-57678-9
    1. Corporate image. 2. Industrial management—Psychological aspects.
3. Social perception. I. Title.

    HD59.2.L49 2005
    659.2—dc22   2005003936

Book design by Charles Sutherland

ISBN 978-0-446-69848-1 (pbk.)

To the champions, the heroic men and women who understand that business is more than the toil for money—it is a demand for excellence. Their rare passion in the cause of commerce inspires all of those inside and out of their enterprise, and to them this book is enthusiastically dedicated.

Acknowledgments

It's been said before, better and more forcefully than I can, that writing a book is not a solitary undertaking. It's encouraged, refined, assisted, and expanded by any number of smart, passionate, inspiring people, who sometimes do the most when they don't realize they're doing anything at all. Such is the process of writing a book, at least for me.

To each of these benevolent witnesses, my gratitude, real and lasting:

Rick Wolff, my determined, diligent editor at Warner Books, whose contributions to the birth of this work were indispensable.

Craig Nelson, my longtime and valued agent and friend, who has watched over my publishing life with the care of a dedicated and experienced surgeon.

Jeffrey Cohen, a smart and valued friend, who continues to encourage my writing.

My LCO-Levine Communications Office staff and associates, headed by Chief Operating Officer Dawn Miller. Staff: Mike Abrams, Clarissa Clarke, Liam Collopy, Shannon

Hartigan, and Brian McWilliams. Associates: Rick Citron, Cindy Carrasco, Phil Kass, Steve Shapiro, and David Weiss.

My closest personal friends, every single one of whom has brightened darkness when life has inevitably cast shadows, but just as often celebrated my victories as if they were their own: Peter Bart, Adam Christing, Craig Hollander, Richard Imprescia, Karen Karsian, Nancy Mager, John McKillop, Mark Miller, Evadne Morakis, Cable Neuhaus, Alyse Reynolds, Tara Kennan, Dr. Robert Kotler, and Lisa Yukelson.

Publishing associates far and wide, who continue to use their formidable skills to prod me to get my ideas into print: Craig Black, Bill Hartley, and Michael Viner.

Contents

graffiti or purse snatching seemed absurd: How would a crackdown on jaywalking lead to a decrease in murders?

The broken windows theory states that something as small and innocuous as a broken window does in fact send a signal to those who pass by every day. If it is left broken, the owner of the building isn't paying attention or doesn't care. That means more serious infractions—theft, defacement, violent crime—might be condoned in this area as well. At best, it signals that no one is watching.

This is the heart of the broken windows theory: Wilson and Kelling write that "social psychologists and police officers tend to agree that if a window in a building is broken and is left unrepaired, all the rest of the windows will soon be broken." Why? Because the message being sent out by a broken window—the *perception* it invites—is that the owner of this building and the people of the community around it don't care if this window is broken: They have given up, and anarchy reigns here. Do as you will, because nobody cares.

Wilson and Kelling suggested that a "broken window"— any small indication that something is amiss and not being repaired—can lead to much larger problems. It sends signals, they said, that the bad guys are in charge here; no one cares about maintaining some kind of order, and anyone who wishes to take advantage of that situation would be unopposed. It leads to lawlessness, a kind of anarchy by neglect.

"Just as physicians now recognize the importance of fostering health rather than simply treating illness, so the police—and the rest of us—ought to recognize the importance of maintaining, intact, communities without broken windows," wrote Wilson and Kelling.

Years later, Wilson told me that the idea behind the broken windows theory "had to do with the responsibility of the police to take seriously small signs of disorder because people were afraid of disorder, and there was a chance disorder could lead to more serious crime." Still, critics of the theory greeted it with skepticism, believing that attention to small infractions would necessarily decrease the amount of attention that could be devoted to much more serious crimes.

The same objection, in slightly less genteel verbiage, was raised when Rudolph Giuliani, the newly elected mayor of New York City in 1994, announced his intention to eliminate graffiti on subway cars and move the hookers and pimps out of Times Square, to make Manhattan more "family-friendly." Critics practically laughed in Giuliani's face, intimating that the "law and order" mayor—who had been elected based largely on his experience as U.S. attorney for the New York area—was dealing with the small crimes because he knew he couldn't contain the larger ones.

They were proved wrong. Giuliani and his new police commissioner, William Bratton, believed that if they sent out clear signals to criminals, and to New York's citizenry generally, that a "zero tolerance" policy would be applied to *all* crime in the city, the result would be a safer, cleaner city. And the statistics bore them out: Over the following few years, the numbers of murders, assaults, robberies, and other violent crimes all went down dramatically. And it had all started with graffiti on subway cars.

I can hear you asking, "What does that have to do with my business? It's all about crime and criminals."

That same theory is applicable to the world of business.

If the restroom at the local Burger King is out of toilet paper, it signals that management isn't paying attention to the needs of its clientele. That could lead the consumer to conclude that the food at this restaurant might not be prepared adequately, that there might be health risks in coming here, or that the entire chain of fast food outlets simply doesn't care about its customers.

Given that scenario, it is not a stretch of the imagination but in fact a point of logic to conclude that the broken windows theory should be applied to business, as it was to the problems of crime in urban areas. Certainly, the perception of the average consumer is a vital part of every business, and if a retailer, service provider, or corporation is sending out signals that its approach is lackadaisical, its methods halfhearted, and its execution indifferent, the business in question could suffer severe—and in some cases, irreparable—losses.

This book is about broken windows in business: how they happen, why they happen, why they are ignored, and the fatal consequences that can result from their being allowed to go unchecked. It is meant as a cautionary tale, a primer, a road map, a manifesto, and a salute to those companies that fix their broken windows promptly. It will explore not only specific examples of broken windows, how they occurred, and what their long-term results were but also the culture that creates an environment in which windows are broken and left unfixed.

I believe that small things make a huge difference in business. The messy condiment area at a fast food restaurant might lead customers to believe the company as a whole doesn't care about cleanliness, and therefore the food itself might be in question. Indifferent help at the counter in an upscale clothing store—even if just one clerk—can signal to the consumer that perhaps standards here aren't as high as they might be (or used to be). An employee at the gas station who wears a T-shirt with an offensive slogan can certainly cause some customers to switch brands of gasoline and lose an enormous company those customers for life.

But that's only the tip of the iceberg. I think we as a society have fostered and encouraged broken windows in our businesses by standing by and letting them happen. If the waiter at a local chain restaurant is impolite, or even merely complacent, about our order, we chalk it up to a bad day, one employee in one outlet of a large chain, and we don't send a letter to management or the corporate level. Even if we do change brands of gasoline after seeing an attendant in an offensive T-shirt, we do not write or e-mail the president of the oil company to alert him to the problem. We are enablers to window breakers in every aspect of every business. We don't even necessarily patronize those companies that fix their broken windows, if the less attentive one is in a more convenient location or has a slightly lower price.

That's not to say we are all to blame when a company has broken windows and doesn't fix them, but it does mean we all bear some responsibility to stand up for what we actually want and have every right to expect out of a company to which we're giving our hard-earned money. In a capitalist society, we can assume that a company that wants to succeed will do its best to fulfill the desires of its consuming public. If the company sees sales slipping but doesn't have data from consumers as to what made them decrease their spending on a retail level, the company will not necessarily know what to fix.

Still, corporations and even small businesses that don't notice and repair their broken windows should not simply be forgiven because their consumers didn't make enough of a fuss. It is the responsibility of the business to tend to its own house. The owner of a Starbucks franchise who decides that revenues are at a healthy level, such that he or she can put off painting the store for another year, is asking for trouble: Yes, things are fine now, but when the paint is faded and peeling and consumers are no longer getting the experience they've come to expect, it will be too late to fix things with, literally, a fresh coat of paint. The time to repair broken windows is the minute they occur.

It's better, however, to prevent such smashed panes of glass to begin with. This book will examine the origins of broken windows with two purposes in mind. First, we will see how the small things that can snowball into large problems develop, so we can best illustrate how to repair the damage once it's been done. But it is equally important to see how these things happen so that a smart business owner can make sure to prevent them at—or before—the very first sign of trouble. If you have a policy to paint the store every year, you'll never have to worry about whether this was the year you waited too long.

In order to best understand how the broken windows theory relates to business, it's important to examine the original theory—as it related to criminal activity—in some detail. Because of the brilliant thinking of Wilson and Kelling, "Broken Windows" illustrated a serious societal problem that was going unnoticed, and helped turn around some of the country's largest cities (including the largest of all) by paying attention to detail.

It began with a program in New Jersey in the mid-1970s. The Safe and Clean Neighborhoods Program was meant to improve the quality of life in twenty-eight Garden State cities, and it was to do so, in part, by increasing the number of police officers on foot patrol, rather than in patrol cars. Police chiefs, Wilson says today, felt that such a move was not likely to lower crime levels, "and the police chiefs were right: They didn't have an effect on crime rates. But they *did* have an effect—and in my view, a powerful effect—on how people felt about their community and their willingness to use it, suggesting that fear of disorder was as important as fear of crime."

Indeed, as Wilson and Kelling wrote in the *Atlantic*, "residents of the foot-patrolled neighborhoods seemed to feel more secure than persons in other areas, tended to believe that crime had been reduced, and seemed to take fewer steps to protect themselves from crime (staying at home with the doors locked, for example). Moreover, citizens in the foot-patrol areas had a more favorable opinion of the police than did those living elsewhere."

What does this all mean to business? It's not likely that having police officers walk the aisles of a Wal-Mart store will increase sales. But it was the *perception* that something was being done to increase order that made the difference for the people living in these New Jersey cities.

In a business (as we'll discuss in detail throughout this book), the broken windows can be literal or metaphorical. Sometimes a broken window really is a broken window, and a new pane of glass needs to be installed as quickly as possible. Most of the time, however, broken windows are the little details, the tiny flaws, the overlooked minutiae, that signal much larger problems either already in place or about to become reality.

We'll examine companies—huge ones, household names—that have failed to notice and repair their broken windows and have suffered greatly for it. We'll also look at those that have made it a priority to attend to every *potentially* broken window and ordered plenty of replacement panes to make quick, seamless repairs. The lessons learned will be many, and varied, and they will have happy and, well, not-so-happy endings. Sometimes companies that deserve to be rebuked for their laziness will go unpunished, but other times there will be retribution at the hands of the public, which shows exactly what happens when you give the people what they *don't* want.

What the public wants more than anything else is to feel that the businesses—retail or service-oriented, consumer or business-to-business—that work for them *care* about what they want. Consumers are looking for businesses that anticipate and fulfill their needs and do so in a way that makes it clear the business understands the consumers' needs or wants and is doing its best to see them satisfied.

Broken windows indicate to the consumer that the business doesn't care—either that it is so poorly run it can't possibly keep up with its obligations or that it has become so oversized and arrogant that it no longer cares about its core consumer. Either of these impressions can be deadly to a business, and we'll see examples of both as we proceed.

If you run a business, and you truly believe that little things don't make a difference, you really should read this book—it may save your business. If you don't run a business but would like to, this can be the road map to your success. If you're merely interested in business and wonder why one succeeds where a very similar one fails, perhaps the examples contained here might help answer that question for you.

But it can't be overemphasized that tiny details—the smaller, the more important—can indeed make a tremendous difference in a business's success or failure. Sometimes, yes, a company can make a huge mistake (the whole New Coke thing was less a broken window than a neutron bomb placed dead center at corporate headquarters), but often, even those are foreshadowed by the little things that go, alas, unnoticed.

A broken window can be a sloppy counter, a poorly located sale item, a randomly organized menu, or an employee with a bad attitude. It can be physical, like a faded, flaking paint job, or symbolic, like a policy that requires consumers to pay for customer service. When the waiter at a Chinese restaurant is named Billy Bob, that's a broken window. When a call for help in assembling a bicycle results in a twenty-minute hold on the phone (playing the same music over and over), that's a broken window. When a consumer asks why she can't return her blouse at the counter and is told, "Because that's the rule," that is a broken window.

They're everywhere. Except at the really sharp businesses. Read on.

Broken
WINDOWS,
Broken
BUSINESS

Chapter One

Broken Windows in Business

The broken windows theory was such a revolutionary, seminal concept in criminal justice that when it was published in 1982, it was considered a complete and total reversal of everything that had come before it. The notion that perception was as important in controlling crime as statistics, that letting "small" crimes slide by was sending a signal not only that the criminals were in charge but that the police were either unwilling or unable to stop them, was laughed at, ridiculed, considered absurd or "radical."

It wasn't until the theory was put into practice in the 1990s on the world's largest stage, in the city of New York, that its seeming simplicity was shown to be genius. Between Mayor Rudolph Giuliani and Police Commissioner William Bratton, the commitment to fixing New York's broken windows—graffiti, fare jumping, squeegee wielding, and the like—might have sounded like an assault on an insignificant annoyance, but it was actually a call to arms, a declaration of war on crime, that proved to be the salvation of a city in crisis. In showing the world that New York City would not tolerate *any* infraction, Giuliani and Bratton were making the larger point that serious law-breakers would be facing much harsher penalties. The good guys *would* be in charge here.

It is a distinction between "law" and "order," one that is important, because it defines what the broken windows theory means and how it will apply to the business world. To adhere to the *law,* one simply manages to live without violating the set code. Simple enough. But to maintain *order* in a city, country, or company, the goal must be to have *everyone* follow the same rules and to make sure that each rule carries the same weight.

To have a rule that says "Thou shalt not murder" and one that says "Don't cross the street against the light" seems like something approaching a contradiction—it sounds like the two infractions shouldn't even be mentioned in the same sentence. But both are rules, both are laws as set up by society. If it is generally accepted that we can violate one, isn't it logical that we could violate the other without any additional fear of punishment?

Rules don't have to be universal, either; they can vary from neighborhood to neighborhood, as the authors of "Broken Windows" discovered when the Newark, New Jersey, police made sure more officers on foot patrol were dispatched as an experiment in the 1970s. In one neighborhood, the foot-patrol officer, whom Wilson and Kelling called Kelly, was careful to enforce the informal, unwritten rules that were set up in that section of the city:

"Drunks and addicts could sit on the stoops, but could not lie down. People could drink on side streets, but not at the main intersection. Bottles had to be in paper bags.

Talking to, bothering, or begging from people waiting at the bus stop was strictly forbidden. If a dispute erupted between a businessman and a customer, the businessman was assumed to be right, especially if the customer was a stranger. If a stranger loitered, Kelly would ask him if he had any means of support and what his business was; if he gave unsatisfactory answers, he was sent on his way. Persons who broke the informal rules, especially those who bothered people waiting at bus stops, were arrested for vagrancy. Noisy teenagers were told to keep quiet."[1]

Wilson and Kelling noted that "these rules were defined and enforced in collaboration with the 'regulars' on the street. Another neighborhood might have different rules, but these, everybody understood, were the rules for *this* neighborhood."

The rules in and of themselves were not exactly revolutionary, nor were they especially strict. There was not a "no tolerance" policy for addicts or alcoholics—they were simply asked to stay in certain areas and to not do certain things in public places. But the rules, as stated, were expected to be enforced, every one.

The same is true in the larger and more dramatic experiment that took place in New York City. When Giuliani and Bratton chose to crack down on graffiti artists, squeegee men, and fare jumpers (those who leap over turnstiles to gain free access to the subway system), they were making the statement that some things that were tolerated before would no longer be acceptable.

It was a calculated expression of control that was meant

---

1. James Q. Wilson and George L. Kelling, "Broken Windows: The Police and Neighborhood Safety," *Atlantic Monthly,* March 1982.

to make a statement not only to those who would spray-paint subway cars or jump over turnstiles—it was also meant (and, it could be argued, *mostly* meant) to be seen by the public.

As Wilson explained to me recently, the police chiefs to whom he and Kelling spoke were actually correct in their expectations that increased foot patrols would not make a difference in the overall crime rate. Where they did have an effect, however—and it was a major one—was on public perception: "on how people felt about their community and their willingness to use it, suggesting that fear of disorder was as important as fear of crime."

Giuliani, speaking to the Conference of Mayors in May 2000, added to that sentiment: "New York City during the 1960s, '70s, '80s and into the early '90s served as a symbol of decline. I keep a national magazine cover describing New York City in 1990 as 'the Rotting Apple,' a city in decline. And at that time, people in the City of New York *accepted it.* They accepted the idea that this was our lot in life: that we were an old city that had seen our greatest days . . . the perception was that things were never going to be as good as they used to be."[2]

Notice that the "perception" of the city's population is what is being mentioned here. The more people saw their city as a place with a glorious past and a mediocre present, the more it became the truth. It wasn't until the little details, the minor infractions, were dealt with that the quality of day-to-day life for citizens of the city showed

---

2. Rudolph W. Giuliani, "Remarks to the Conference of Mayors on Restoring Accountability in City Government," May 9, 2000, as delivered. Italics mine.

noticeable improvement, and at that point, real change could be achieved.

Now, how does this apply to business?

The broken windows theory is all about the unmistakable power of perception, about what people see and the conclusions they draw from it. It doesn't claim that cracking down on graffiti will lead to fewer murders; in fact, crime rates overall are not necessarily affected by the theory being put into practice, as Wilson himself acknowledged. What is important is that as the quality of life in these areas improved, even on a scale that might seem insignificant, the population began feeling better about its surroundings, and *that* led to significant change: People spent more time out of their homes, participating in events and patronizing local businesses.

In business, perception is even more critical. The way a customer (or potential customer) *perceives* your business is a crucial element in your success or failure. Make one mistake, have one rude employee, let that customer walk away with a negative experience *one time,* and you are inviting disaster.

I work in the public relations business in Hollywood. I have represented Barbra Streisand, Charlton Heston, Linda Evans, Fleetwood Mac, Vanna White, Demi Moore, Michael J. Fox, Robert Evans, and Michael Jackson, among many others. I understand the power of perception, and believe me, it can be devastatingly powerful—for good or for bad.

Perception is also something that happens in the blink of an eye. There is nothing more fleeting than a first impression; it is made in a heartbeat. But a perception can be made at any time, even after you have been acquainted with a person or company for years. And opinions turn on such perceptions.

For example, let's say you have bought your coffee at the same store every day for the past five years on your way to work in the morning. You've gone there unfailingly, sometimes added a bagel or muffin, and occasionally stopped in at lunchtime. The counter staff knows your name, knows your usual order, and can anticipate your preferences.

But one day, even without thinking about it, you happen to notice as you stand in line waiting to order that the walls haven't been painted in years. There are slight cracks and chips in the paint just behind the counter help. It's never occurred to you before, but that small perception makes a difference.

Maybe you start to wonder if those paint chips aren't falling into the coffee or onto a surface where rolls and bagels are cut and prepared for sale. Perhaps the fact that you noticed the paint job makes you realize just how long you've been waiting on line every morning. It's just possible that you consider which other aspects of the store's physical plant—including its cleanliness—might be in disrepair. You might end up by wondering exactly why you've been frequenting this particular business all along.

That one little perception can pack an extraordinary wallop, can't it?

Now, nothing assumed in this scenario is necessarily true: There's no reason to think the coffee outlet's cleanliness, commitment to service, sanitary conditions, or food preparation are at all in question. But you perceived one flaw, and from that allowed your mind to wander into territories it might not have ventured without some direction.

It's not a place the owner would want his customers to go. And if he takes care of broken windows like the paint job, he can avoid such mental journeys. It's better to create a *positive* perception, of course, but avoiding the negative ones is far and away the most critical thing one can do to attract and keep customers. There is no alternative for an unbroken window, other than one that is under repair.

Let this book be your manifesto, your obsession, your bible of perception. From this moment on, consider how everything *seems* to your customers, your employees, the public in general. Yes, you have to care about what really *is*, but you also have to concern yourself with the way things *appear* to be.

It doesn't matter if you tell a suspicious customer about your scrupulous cleaning techniques, your patented methods for keeping the food away from anything that might fall on it, or your plan to speed up counter lines. Mostly, it doesn't matter because the customer *isn't ever going to tell you about her concerns;* she's just not coming back to your store again. Generally speaking, consumers will not voice their complaints. (I know, you've heard plenty of bitching and will argue with me, but the truth is that the vast majority of those who find something wrong will not communicate that perception to you—they'll just stop being a customer.)

The thing about a broken window is that it's not always obvious. The owner of the coffee outlet in this scenario isn't necessarily someone who doesn't care about his business or is given to outrageously lax upkeep. This is someone who either didn't notice that his paint job was starting to erode or felt that by waiting another year to paint he could save some operating capital, and besides, sales were consistent and the customers hadn't complained. There are other, squeakier wheels to grease.

Unfortunately, that is the attitude that can sound a death knell for a business, but on a frequency the human ear can't detect. Let things slip, let the clientele notice things you haven't, and you might as well throw a Molotov cocktail into your store and start from scratch: Your business is on its way out. Constant vigilance, an absolute obsession with detail, is essential to running a business today, particularly one that deals directly with the public (although we will be considering business-to-business broken windows as well).

If you're not obsessed with the details of your business, you can believe me, there will be someone who *is* obsessed with his, and he will see to it that he overruns your customer rolls and decimates the loyalty you've built up with your regular clientele. Show the slightest chink in the armor you've built up, and an exposed weakness will become the most obvious flaw you can imagine. Your business, to put it simply, will not survive too many broken windows. And "too many" is "one."

Consider the case of Martha Stewart. Was Ms. Stewart convicted of insider trading? Fraud? Tampering with a public trust? No. She was convicted of wrongdoings involved with *covering up* whatever alleged improprieties had gone on. Why was she trying to cover up? Because she was concerned about the *perception* that her business was unscrupulous and that she, personally, was not trustworthy. Obsession with detail? Perhaps, but far too late. You can't fix a broken window by throwing rocks through all the others.

Many a politician has been brought down not by ac-
cusers who had solid evidence that the official had done
something illegal or unscrupulous, but by the effort to
suppress the *perception* that might have come from the
allegation itself. History is littered with the carcasses of
officials who were discarded after trying to cover up
something that might not have been as serious a scandal
had it been dealt with quickly and efficiently—and publicly.

A broken window, make no mistake, is best repaired
before it breaks. The most desirable scenario is to fix the
problem before it is visible, and never to have to consider
perception, because there will be nothing to perceive. But
if a flaw arises, the only course of action—the *only* course
—is to deal with it immediately, to do so without trying to
put a cosmetic sheen on it, and to make sure it is, without
question, repaired. A piece of masking tape on a cracked
window might prevent it from breaking, but it will be visible for all to see and will have the same perceived effect
as a broken window itself. Repairs must be complete and
immediate.

But what constitutes a broken window in business? It's
easy to spot the physical ones, like the peeling paint on a
wall, but what about the less obvious problems? What
about employees who don't follow the company's stated
policies and present a flawed, incorrect picture to the consuming public? How can you deal with a broken window
when you're in corporate headquarters and there are thirty
thousand outlets to oversee?

Well, consider the case of the world's largest restaurant
chain. Its broken windows have come very close to bringing down the house. The last chapter in this story has yet
to be written, but the fact that it was ever in question is a

testament to the power of broken windows and how far the mighty can fall. Indeed, consider the case of McDonald's, which once was considered (and considered itself) invincible, and see what broken windows can do, even to a giant.

PERCEPTION VS. REALITY

- It is your customer's *perception* of your business that will dictate his or her level of loyalty to your business. Make one mistake, and you can damage that perception.

- Little things mean a lot. If you notice that the carpet on the floor at your dentist's office is a little worn, you might find yourself wondering whether the dental instruments have been replaced recently.

- Broken windows are best repaired before they break.

- It's the cover-up that gets you—don't make excuses for broken windows or deny that they're broken. Take your hit, own up to the problem, and fix it.

- Obsession to detail is essential. There is no substitute.

Chapter Two

Can McDonald's Be Saved?

For those born during or after the 1950s, a world without McDonald's is just short of unthinkable. The golden arches making up the hamburger behemoth's logo create a symbol so ubiquitous, so huge, so utterly pervasive, that the thought of it vanishing from the street, let alone the world, is practically laughable.

But it could happen someday. And why? Because the huge company has neglected its broken windows, and the public has taken notice.

Despite its presence in virtually every country, on every continent, in almost every town in the United States, McDonald's is not the paragon of customer satisfaction or brand integrity it once was. In fact, consumers are fed up with Mickey D's indifference toward them, its abandonment of its core principles, and its obvious contempt for those who patronize its tens of thousands of stores.

Consider this: The American Customer Satisfaction Index (ACSI) is compiled each year from quarterly surveys made by the University of Michigan's National Quality Research Center, in conjunction with the American Society for Quality, a Milwaukee institute, and CFI Group, a consulting firm based in Ann Arbor, Michigan. In February 2003, it was reported that for the tenth year in a row, McDonald's had scored below average—and significantly so—for the fast food industry.

On the 100-point scale used by the ACSI, McDonald's score was 61, down over 1.5 points from a similar survey done a year earlier. And the company's average score was 5 to 10 points below the industry average since 1994, according to the ACSI.

Among the questions the sixteen thousand consumers surveyed answered were evaluations of the outlet's food, its service, and whether the order was handled correctly.

The same time period's survey results saw Taco Bell's scores go up 1.5 points, Domino's Pizza up 2.7 percent, Wendy's up 2.8 percent, and chief rival Burger King's scores up 4.6 percent, a good 7 points higher than McDonald's.

Bad enough? Wait: A *Fortune* magazine article of April 2002 showed a sixth consecutive quarter of "disappointing profits" for McDonald's. The stock price took a good number of hits, and there were wholesale changes in the executive suites at the company's Oak Brook, Illinois, headquarters. In 2004, the purveyor of the Big Mac with Cheese was announcing it would eliminate the "supersize" option from its stores, calling the process "menu simplification."

All right, so McDonald's, one of the world's largest corporations, is going through a rough time. Well, what does that have to do with *your* business? If you sell hamburgers, french fries, or sodas, you might *welcome* the collapse of a behemoth competitor like McDonald's.

Well, if something of this magnitude can happen to McDonald's because it is failing to fix its broken windows, can't the same thing happen to you, no matter what business you might be in, if you don't see to the small things that make all the difference?

What is especially puzzling about McDonald's is that the company's core philosophy would seem to stand for exactly the kind of attention to detail and basic service that seems to be lacking in its practice. The corporation's headquarters boasts a posted list of promises made to consumers that *must* be kept, under any circumstances. Among them are fast service and clean facilities, two areas that were cited by consumers as lacking in McDonald's restaurants during the ACSI survey.

By contrast, Papa John's, the pizza chain with far fewer outlets than McDonald's, is at the top of the fast food industry (which likes to call itself "rapid service") in consumer satisfaction and has been consistently so for a few years. With a score of 78 in the 2002 survey, Papa John's not only came in first among fast food restaurants but was also the only such chain to beat the retail sector average and do so for a number of years in a row.

McDonald's, it was noted by the ACSI, ranked last in its category and among *all retail outlets* for the eighth consecutive year.

In fact, the American Society for Quality quoted its past president, Jack West, as saying that "the greatest weakness for McDonald's is service quality. People go to McDonald's for a combination of fast service, consistent products, low price and convenience. Obviously, McDonald's is not consistently meeting those expectations."

Roots of the Problem

Granted, some of McDonald's troubles were not directly the fault of the company itself. An epidemic of mad cow disease in 2001 and 2002 caused some panic, particularly in Europe, regarding eating beef, and that certainly didn't help the sales in hamburger outlets. Globally and in the United States, economic lethargy meant jobs being cut, fewer people eating in restaurants, and slower sales. Concerns about cholesterol and heart disease led to a decrease in the consumption of beef overall. These things were outside McDonald's control, although the corporation was capable of responding to some of them, a subject we'll touch upon a bit later.

The point is, those outside concerns were not the main reasons for McDonald's decline in customer satisfaction, which led directly to decreased sales. (The corporation announced closings of its outlets in a number of countries, something that would have been unthinkable just a few years ago.) The University of Michigan study of consumer satisfaction found in 2001 that 11 percent of McDonald's customers were dissatisfied with their visit on any given day. Close to 70 percent of those dissatisfied customers were even more disgruntled following some contact with the company, because the complaints were not handled to the customer's satisfaction. And here's the part that really tells the story: *More than half of all dissatisfied customers cut back on their visits to McDonald's and told as many as ten other people about their experience.*

McDonald's brand contract, stated in its headquarters and at all its outlets in writing, states that the brand vision is "to be the world's best quick service restaurant experience," which is to include outstanding service, quality, value, cleanliness, and "having every customer in every restaurant smile." If eleven out of every one hundred people who walk in aren't smiling on the way out, are angry about the way their complaints are received, and might become less frequent visitors, there is something wrong.

According to the University of Michigan study, the top five complaints by McDonald's customers were rude employees, not having Happy Meal toys, slow service, missing items or receiving the wrong order, and unclean restaurants. All of these points of contention fly directly in the face of McDonald's stated goals, their most basic promises made to consumers.

These are all broken windows, and they are not being repaired. In fact, as is the case with most broken windows, more glass is being shattered while the first cracks still await attention.

It starts, clearly, with something as seemingly insignificant as an inadequate supply of toys to go with Happy Meals, the prepackaged products aimed at young children. Because McDonald's does a great deal of advertising and promotion to children, and emphasizes the Happy Meal toy in all of it, children will often ask to be taken to the restaurant specifically to get that particular toy. When the franchise owner or manager has not ordered an adequate number of toys, or the company itself has failed to produce enough and supply its restaurants, the child is disappointed, the parent frustrated, and the cycle of dissatisfaction set in motion.

But the broken windows at McDonald's are much more plentiful than the absence of expected toys. For adults, they are often so obvious and numerous that a discussion of them seems superfluous, but they are worth examining.

Come Back, Ray!

It is my contention that if Ray Kroc, who bought the McDonald's name and system and built the corporation almost single-handedly into one of the largest companies in the world, were to rise from the grave and walk into a present-day McDonald's franchise, he would die a second, more painful death.

From embarrassment.

In many locations, the cleanliness and efficiency Kroc so diligently guarded are nonexistent. The condiment areas are not cleaned regularly. The counter help is, at best, indifferent. The bathrooms . . . well, let's stay out of the bathrooms.

Key points are the ones that Ray Kroc emphasized a half century ago: dependable quality; fast, accommodating service (it doesn't have to be "friendly," but it sure as hell should be "polite"); a clean, comfortable place to eat; and value for the working people who make up the over-whelming majority of McDonald's customers.

On the surface, that doesn't seem like such a tall order: The company should just go back to Kroc's principles and then enforce them strictly. But it's not that simple. The world isn't the same today as when Kroc walked into a San Bernardino hamburger stand in 1954.

The broken windows at McDonald's are not all that different from those in other large businesses that have seen their star power decline in recent years. But when the business is based on speed and consumer satisfaction, and both of those begin to erode at the same time, the prognosis is not good. McDonald's needs to get in touch with its inner Ray Kroc, and fast.

And if it can happen to them, it can happen to you. Think about it.

DESERVE A BREAK?

- Customer loyalty is a wonderful thing to have, but customer *stupidity* should not be expected. Customers won't stick with you if you stick it to them.

- Core values—the things that a business promises its customers—are never to be taken for granted. If you make a promise to consumers and don't keep it, you are asking for bankruptcy.

- The little things that plague McDonald's aren't the quality of the food or the promises the company makes. They are the promises *not* kept—the dirty bathrooms, the absent Happy Meal toys. Customers are disgruntled because they've been told to expect something and then are given less.

- Broken windows can be repaired, but they have to be seen and fixed as quickly as possible.

Chapter Three

Obsession and Compulsion

Some people suffer from a condition known as OCD, obsessive-compulsive disorder. Its symptoms may include an incredibly focused interest in one topic or the inability to function without certain rituals, like frequently washing hands or locking doors over and over. These people often seek treatment and can sometimes lead what is considered a normal life through therapy, medication, or other avenues.

While in personal life OCD is a challenge, in business, obsession and compulsion are *good* things. In fact, they are necessary. Without an obsessive attention to detail and a compulsive drive to fix broken windows in a business, disaster is being courted. In today's business climate, everyone should have OCD concerning broken windows.

And no window is too small to break; nor is any break too small to repair. Everything counts, significantly more than you might think.

The concepts of obsession and compulsion are central

to the idea of broken windows. I can't stress strongly enough how important it is to have a driving, obsessive fixation on your business, and a compulsion to see everything done in the right way every single time. Repairing what mistakes are made along the way can't be an optional thing; it has to be an absolute, unquestioned necessity that would literally cause you to lose sleep were it not taken care of immediately and completely.

Obsession

Obsession is the fixation on one idea, subject, or concept. It allows virtually no other thoughts and becomes an all-consuming, all-important idea in the mind. It would not be an exaggeration to say that in order to prevent and repair all broken windows, you must be—not *should* be, not *may* be, but *must* be—obsessed with your business.

You have to feel personally affronted if something goes wrong with your business. And that "something" can be *anything*. The idea that a trash can hasn't been emptied, that a counter hasn't been cleaned, needs to be a personal insult, an abomination. You have to feel physically ill if you find a problem in your business, no matter how small and (here's a word I use with great caution) insignificant it might seem.

Nothing is small, and absolutely nothing is insignificant.

It's not enough to be concerned about your business; it's not enough to be interested in its success. You have to be obsessed, or you are inviting disaster. If you're not lying in bed at night trying to think of ways to improve business, to serve your customers better, and to fix the broken windows you have or will have soon, you are not doing your job properly. And that fervor must be communicated to every single employee you have. It's not enough for *you* to be obsessed—*everyone* who works for the company must be equally single-minded.

There are few companies as well entrenched in the American landscape these days as Starbucks. The company that convinced the world that a four-dollar cup of coffee is not ridiculous has a presence on what seems like every corner, has become part of the language, and now sells coffee in supermarkets, convenience stores, and bodegas in addition to its own stores. Its service is still considered exemplary, and its product is being accepted by people the world over. It's hard to imagine that things could get much better for Starbucks.

Indeed, even the company's chairman, Howard Schultz, believes Starbucks is doing as well as it can do. He has warned his investors that the current sales performance can't be sustained indefinitely. But he knows where the windows that might be broken are, and he has a plan to keep them crack-free.

Schultz increased the paid training time for the company's "most motivated employees" by as much as a third, to thirty-two hours, in early 2004. His plan was to make the employees better educated about coffee generally and, by extension, better at selling more brewed coffee and bags of whole beans. He wanted to make sure that customers entering a Starbucks would be met by employees who knew their product inside and out, and could discuss it, recommend choices, and answer questions as well as anyone in the industry.

That's impressive, and it is also a sign of obsession. Schultz understands that Starbucks has expanded rapidly and that such growth often presages a fall. Companies like Boston Market, Crazy Eddie, and Kmart have all suffered from too much too soon. Schultz wants to ensure that no such thing would happen to the upscale coffee chain in his charge.

His choice—to improve the Starbucks brand by improving its employees' knowledge of the product—is a bold move. It shows obsession on his part, and it demands obsession on the part of those who work for the chain. By knowing as much as they can possibly know about their product, Starbucks employees must cross over from interested to obsessed with coffee, and they must demonstrate this obsession to their customers by exhibiting the level of education and training they have received. It's a fine line to walk, as the employees must know how to be helpful and knowledgeable without being irritating know-it-alls.

Obsession is a dangerous tool. It's essential, but it has to be handled properly to be effective. Yes, the customer base should be made aware of your total commitment to service, but you can't demonstrate it in such an overbearing fashion that it becomes obnoxious.

How obsessed must you be? Keep in mind that Ray Kroc used to grab a mop and clean up when he visited a McDonald's he felt wasn't up to snuff. Rudolph Giuliani didn't rest until every New York City subway car was free of graffiti. CEOs hire mystery shoppers to report on the state of their retail outlets, then go into the stores themselves and double-check what the mystery shoppers have reported. It's not enough to demand that something be done—you have to make sure that it is done by checking *yourself.*

The saying that a chain is as strong as its weakest link has great resonance in the world of the broken windows for business theory. An employee—especially one who has direct contact with customers—is the most visible type of broken window imaginable. Nothing will drive customers away faster than an employee who isn't with the program.

Service is the absolute center of broken windows for business. Your product might very well be the best in the world, but if it's being sold and represented by employees who with every word and action betray their complete indifference toward the customer and the customer's needs, you will fail, without question. Indeed, if the first employee to come into contact with the customer (counter help in a retail setting, the receptionist in a doctor's office, etc.) is not the best possible face for your business, you have a broken window that could very easily shatter your business very quickly.

Become obsessed with your hiring practices, since it is much more difficult, expensive, and damaging to hire a bad employee and then be forced into a firing situation. Know ahead of time what kind of person you need, and then take steps to hire one with the proper knowledge for the job and the proper *attitude* to exhibit that knowledge. Hire the obsessed, but hire the obsessed who can relate to customers if the employee is going to have any contact with your clientele at all.

Obsession is not just a line of perfume—it's a tool, and

a valuable one. Without it, you will be operating at a disadvantage, and in business today, you need every single advantage you can get. Eat, drink, and sleep your business. Worry about it. Load up on antacids. It's not going to be an easy ride, but you can make it a successful one if you're obsessed enough.

Compulsion

There is a very clear line between obsession and compulsion. Where obsession demands merely an intense, focused interest on all aspects of your business, compulsion requires more practice. It is just as powerful and just as essential a concept as obsession, but it relies more on instinct and conditioned responses than thought and planning. Compulsion is to obsession what lust is to love.

It's one thing to like your living room to be neat; it's quite another to be incapable of leaving the room if everything is not in exactly the proper place. Compulsive behavior means that you are paralyzed if things aren't precisely the way you have decided they should be. Watch the television series *Monk* and you'll get the idea: The character might be investigating a horrible murder, but he can't really concentrate on the clues if the shades on the windows aren't all lowered to the same level. That's compulsion: the involuntary need to have things be a certain way.

In business, compulsion is as useful a tool as exists on the planet. It is perfect to help fix broken windows, as it will not allow you to even consider going on with your day until that window has been repaired. Compulsion implies a stubbornness, a devotion to detail and order, that goes far beyond what most businesspeople believe to be sufficient, even excessive.

Compulsion means not ever letting a customer see a bathroom that isn't spotless. It means never letting someone stay on hold with a voice mail system for more than one minute before contact with a real human being. It means not one employee who isn't going to say "please" and "thank you" to every customer, no matter what the circumstances. Compulsion is all about consistency, since it tolerates nothing outside the established order, and it requires all repairs to be made immediately.

George Steinbrenner III is not the most popular employer on the planet. In fact, he is legendary for being demanding and uncompromising with his employees, from the parking lot attendant to the $25-million-a-year Yankee third baseman. Nothing is ever good enough, and nothing escapes Steinbrenner's notice. If something is going on at Yankee Stadium, the man everyone calls the Boss knows about it. If that something is not what the Boss wants, it is changed—*now*.

Steinbrenner's insistence on having enough bathrooms in the stadium, a building that existed for fifty years before he owned the team that plays there, has been well documented. He knows about the ushers showing people to their seats, he knows about the concession stand employees, he understands the grounds crew and what it must do, and he certainly oversees the players and on-field management.

"Buying the Yankees is like buying the *Mona Lisa*,"

Steinbrenner has said. "You don't put the *Mona Lisa* into a cheap frame and hide it in the closet."

Some of the rules imposed on all Yankee employees—no beards; suits and ties whenever traveling in public—are cosmetic, but they are imposed from on high, from the Boss himself (who, it must be pointed out, often wears turtlenecks). Steinbrenner knows that image is important to perception and that the perception of his product, which happens to be a baseball team made up of men, is essential to ticket sales and other revenue streams. He makes sure that every detail is attended to, and when one is not, he fixes that broken window immediately.

When, on occasion, one of his players has defied the "no beards" policy during the baseball season, or let his hair grow to lengths the Boss felt was not in keeping with the Yankees' image, that player—no matter how beloved, well paid, or integral to the team's success—was disciplined. Image was maintained, and perception was consistent.

Is this a sign of a compulsive nature? In business, it should be. A broken window allowed to stay broken—even if there is every intention of fixing it eventually—is the wrong sign to the outside world. It tells passersby that no one is in charge here and no one cares what happens. That is the death knell of any business, and it simply can't be tolerated. If that means you have to be compulsive, then be compulsive.

When it doesn't come naturally, compulsion is a practiced art. Train yourself to notice the broken windows and then act on them immediately. Refuse to move on to the next item on the agenda until that window is repaired, or until the mechanism to repair it is in place and operating properly. If the broken window is an employee, or a policy of the company, deal with it as quickly and efficiently as possible and make sure that every company employee is aware of the move. People can't be expected to comply with a rule they have not been informed about.

Swift, decisive action is essential in fixing broken windows. Every day that goes by without visible action is a signal that the engineer is asleep at the switch and anarchy rules. It is important, even if the window can't be fixed at this moment, to erect a sign that reads "Broken window being repaired." That can be a literal, physical sign when the broken window is a physical flaw, and it can be a metaphorical, implied signal when the broken window is a policy that needs revamping or a change in the company's direction.

Still, compulsion is as useful a tool as obsession, if not an even more useful one, because it does demand swift action. If you are not able to move on until you are satisfied that a problem is being solved, you will be sure to solve that problem quickly. The key is in planning; the idea is to train yourself to notice the broken windows when, or before, they occur and to deal with them as fast as you can. Many large companies have found themselves in extremely difficult circumstances when they did not act compulsively.

Obsessive/Compulsive Order

- In the world of business, it is a positive thing to be obsessive and compulsive. It's the only way to successfully avoid and repair broken windows that can lead to disaster.

- *Nothing* is insignificant. There is no such thing in business. If it's wrong, and it can be right, it *must* be made right. If you tell yourself that no one will notice, someone *will* notice—and you'll never see that customer again.

- It's not enough to be obsessed yourself: You must hire the obsessed as well. You can't be everywhere at all times, but you can hire people who are, and they have to be just as irrationally dedicated to perfection as you are.

- Compulsive behavior feeds the image of no-defects performance you're trying to cultivate. It is never enough to be dedicated to doing well; it has to become a reflex action.

- In most aspects of life, obsession and compulsion can be debilitating or at least inconvenient. In business, they are useful tools. Cultivate them.

Chapter Four

How the Mighty Have Fallen

In the 1980s and '90s, few symbols were as recognizable in this country as the Kmart logo. When the chain reached its all-time high of 2,323 stores in 1994, there appeared to be a Kmart on every highway, in every shopping mall, virtually around every bend in the road. So when Kmart announced in 2002, its fortieth-anniversary year, that it was seeking bankruptcy protection and that it would close stores in forty-four states and Puerto Rico as part of its reorganization plan, the news came as a shock.

It shouldn't have.

"Kmart's dismal bottom line is directly related to its lack of customer service and its out-of-control operating costs," says John Tschohl, an international management consultant and speaker. "If the company had taken just 10 percent of its advertising or renovation budgets and used that money to train its employees in the art of customer service, Kmart might have realized profits similar to those of Wal-Mart."[1]

---

1. http://teamapproach.com/kmart.asp.

Poor customer service is the ultimate broken window. It is the thing that all consumers will notice immediately, that will make an enormous negative impact and that will not only hurt the company offering the service but give consumers strong incentive to patronize its competition. And demonstrable customer service problems will not only convince consumers that the company doesn't care about its own business—the message of broken windows throughout the business world—they will make an even more damaging point: that the company doesn't care about its *customers,* either. That will kill a business faster and more completely than any other oversight.

Kmart grew from the S. S. Kresge chain and opened its first store in 1962, the same year Sam Walton opened the first Wal-Mart. Today, while Kmart does its best to emerge from bankruptcy by merging with Sears, Wal-Mart is the world's largest retailer. Where did the paths separate, and why so dramatically?

In January 2002, George Chamberlin wrote in the San Diego–area *North County Times:* "Five years ago, the betting money might have favored Kmart. They had just signed up an exclusive distribution contract with Martha Stewart, a sure magnet for baby boomers. And supermodels like Kathy Ireland and Jaclyn Smith were hawking merchandise every Sunday in the Kmart newspaper supplements. At the same time, Wal-Mart was pursuing a different strategy: position the company as the place to shop if you want to save money. Advertising was designed to build a corporate image, not sell specific products. At the same time, Wal-Mart started aggressively selling food products and today is the largest grocery store chain in the United States."[2]

Chamberlin also noted that while Wal-Mart made sure to place its stores in high-traffic, shopper-friendly locations, Kmart was more interested in saving money on rent. Kmart is a classic example of what I call *Broken Windows Hubris*, the unfortunate—and destructive—tendency in some huge corporations (and some less enormous) to believe that they are so successful, so large, so invincible, so much a part of modern society, that they are not subject to the same scrutiny by the public that makes any other company answerable to the broken windows theory. These companies—and among them are McDonald's, Sears, and Disney—suffer from attacks of ego, yes, but that's too simple an explanation. The type of miscalculation we're discussing here is much more pervasive, from the CEO to the janitor; it is the overwhelming perception from within the company that *nothing can ever bring us down because we're just too good.*

Kmart's Broken Windows Hubris was evident in its blasé customer service; in prices that weren't the lowest in town; in policies that seemed to make sense, but really demonstrated how little the company cared about its customer base.

The truth is, Kmart's problems began long before Target and Wal-Mart began to overtake it in sales and in the public's perception. And keep in mind that the public's perception of a company might be more important than the truth, since the truth, if it is not what the public believes, can't really set you free.

---

2. www.nctimes.com/news/2002/20020123/85214.html.

Consider how many people truly believed that Procter & Gamble had some kind of ties with satanic cults, due to a symbol on some of the company's products, which was rumored to be linked to such groups. While the rumors bore no truth whatsoever, it was a public relations nightmare to reverse that perception in the public's mind. The company, with some extremely aggressive and well-planned public relations tactics, did manage to get out the message that the rumors were utterly groundless, but it cost P&G a good deal of money, and it still requires some public relations maintenance to this day.

In Kmart's case, the problems were considerably more pervasive and the windows broken at a much more basic level. The covenant made with the public—that Kmart would be the place for low prices and quality merchandise—was not maintained. The trademark Blue Light Specials, which could be activated at any time in a Kmart store and represented unusually deep price cuts on a particular item for a limited time, underlined this point for the consumer. In other words, there was always the possibility that a product—*any* product—could be had for a very low price in a Kmart store. Low prices were the point. By making sure that the price cuts were seemingly random and that the base of products sold in Kmart stores was very broad, Kmart made sure the public was getting the message: "We have what you want, and we are selling it at the lowest possible price." It also pushed the point that it was *exciting* to shop at Kmart, because you never knew when a terrific bargain might be offered.

How, then, did Kmart reach a point where it closed six hundred stores and cut 67,000 jobs between January 2002 and May 2003, when it emerged from Chapter 11 protection? How did it manage to lose $3.22 *billion* in 2002, even as it became leaner and meaner, cutting its size by almost 33 percent?

Kmart lost sight of its covenant with the consumer. It stopped offering Blue Light Specials because the company saw itself as something other than a discount retailer. Because of Broken Windows Hubris, the boardroom became tired of "Blue Light Special" being a late-night comedian's punch line and of having the company seen as something akin to the tiny chains around the country that sold all items for a dollar. Kmart, in short, wanted respect, and in seeking it, lost the consumer's trust. It was the wrong trade to make, and it cost the company dearly.

Clearly, this was a company that wasn't listening to its customers. If customer service had been a priority with Kmart at that point, it might have saved its business and its market share. Then again, if customer service had been a priority with Kmart from the beginning, it might not have found itself in this predicament to begin with.

What Kmart hadn't learned was that consumers make or break a retail business. The ultimate broken window—customer service difficulties—will overwhelm any marketing plan, even deep discounts. People simply want their retail businesses to serve the customer, not the business, and without that component, no retailer of any product is going to survive for long.

American Airlines, once the country's largest and seemingly most invincible airline, came within inches of bankruptcy in 2003, surviving only because its unions agreed to last-minute concessions that kept the company out of Chapter 11 protection. An upstart that emphasizes customer service above all other things, jetBlue was thriving at the same time. Consumers want to be treated better, and businesses only sporadically notice or act on that desire. It's the reason Nordstrom has a pianist on staff full-time and offers impeccable customer service. It's the reason no L. L. Bean customer will ever end an encounter with that company unsatisfied if the company has a say in the matter (and it does).

Apple Computer holds a small fraction of the market share for its industry, perhaps 4 or 5 percent. Microsoft dominates its industry, eating up market share and dictating to the rest of the world what programs will and will not be run on the vast majority of the world's personal computers. But Apple users are never disgruntled; they are almost exclusively described in the press as "enthusiasts," while the computing world in general detests the policies of Microsoft and particularly its customer service. Does this constitute a dichotomy? Does it disprove the idea that the company with superior customer service will prevail? Does it mean that broken windows in business don't really mean that much?

Not at all. While Microsoft's policies do alienate some consumers, its products deliver precisely what the company promises they will deliver. Microsoft does not make the mistake of Kmart, trying to be something it is not in order to attract a minority of consumers. But Apple, which does appeal to a smaller percentage of the public, *knows* it is a niche market. Surely, the company's board of directors would be thrilled if the vast majority of consumers decided to pay higher prices for a more elegant system and friendly customer service. But Mac enthusiasts are just that—enthusiasts—and they are among the most loyal consumers on this planet.

The lessons of Kmart are many, but the key is in this area: Poor customer service, the ultimate broken window, coupled with an unrealistic view of the company from within (Broken Windows Hubris), will sink a company, no matter how large and ubiquitous it may once have been. Kmart tried to fix its broken windows by covering them over with clear plastic, but the shattered glass beneath could still be seen by the consuming public, and as of this writing, it is still visible.

What Went Wrong

- A company that believes itself to be too big and powerful to worry about customer service suffers from Broken Windows Hubris, and unless it changes its ways, it will come to no good end.

- Not paying more attention to customer service than to anything else is business suicide.

- When sales start to slip or business is not what it once was, blaming the consumer is not only counterproductive, it's ridiculous. There is no point to saying that the wrong people are buying your product or service—the effort should go into providing the best possible experience for the person who is doing the buying, and catering your whole business to that consumer.

- Trying to find a new consumer instead of servicing the loyal customers you have is Broken Windows Hubris at its most destructive.

- Never assume you are smarter or more sophisticated than your customer. If you think you need to *explain* your business to the customer, perhaps you need the customer to explain your business to you.

- You can't fix a broken window by hiding it. A cracked pane of glass covered in clear plastic will still show the damage. Real repairs must be made, and made quickly, when a broken window is discovered.

Chapter Five

Expectation vs. Reality

When you walk into a movie theater, would you expect to walk out with a free book?

Some East Coast moviegoers who went to Loews theaters in April 2004 were given a promotional copy of "teaser" chapters from two books by best-selling author Harlan Coben in a professionally bound paperback edition with a slick cover. Yes, it was a promotional item and could be seen as advertising, but it was hardly a throwaway flyer or coupon. It felt like a real book. People took it home and read it.

Will some of them spend twenty-five dollars for a hardcover edition of one of the books? Perhaps. But all of them will remember that they went to the movies and came home with a little something extra.

That's an example of the difference between expectation (seeing a movie) and reality (being given a book). Other examples—even easier to implement and which the consumer is probably not expecting—include saying "hello," "thank you," "please," and "you're welcome." Two of the biggest words to say in order to avoid broken windows—and, perhaps, give a customer a new idea of what reality can and should be: "I'm sorry."

Every time a customer or client calls or enters your business, that customer has an expectation. Depending on the nature of your business, that expectation might be a quality product, excellent service, help with a problem, or simply the presence of a product the consumer has always relied upon. If that expectation is met, the customer will be satisfied, although probably not overwhelmed. If the expectation is not met, or if the personnel fulfilling it are not helpful or courteous, the customer will walk away with a negative impression of your business, and you may have lost a customer—for life.

But consider another possibility: You might *exceed* your customer's expectation. Maybe you'll deliver more than he or she anticipated, be just a little bit more courteous, more helpful, friendlier. Maybe you'll put in extra effort and make it show; or simply put in the extra effort so that the negative things that *could* show don't ever materialize. Train employees to always say "please" and "thank you" and to take responsibility when they do something wrong, to apologize for mistakes or inconveniences. Do more than the competition.

Now, suppose you did all that by design.

It seems like the most basic, simplest rule a business could have: *exceed expectations.* But the vast majority of businesses today would be hard-pressed simply to *meet* expectations, let alone surpass them. If the broken windows for business theory teaches anything, it should be that *the customer may not always be right, but customers certainly always think they are, and if you agree with them, you are all on your way to exceeding their expectations.*

"Our expectation is to meet and exceed the customer's anticipation," says Steve Shapiro, vice president of entertainment services for City National Bank in Los Angeles. "When little things go wrong, it drives me nuts, because they didn't have to go wrong."

Think about your experiences as a consumer. When you're dealing with a small retail or service business today, you are rarely greeted with a smile. You are, in fact, rarely greeted at all. At best, you are met with a tolerant gaze and asked (if you're lucky), "Can I help you?" The honest answer is usually, "I've been wondering that myself."

Dealing with a large corporation can be even worse. Call one sometime and have a stopwatch handy. See how long it takes for you to speak to a living, breathing human being after you're done with all the automated phone system prompts. Press 1, press 2, press 3, and still, you're listening to endless minutes of Kenny G interrupted only by a computer voice telling you how important your call is to the company that's kept you on hold now for ten minutes without even knowing what your problem is.

During the 2000 presidential campaign, Ralph Nader was fond of saying that if he was working late at the office and wanted to listen to classical music, he'd call United Airlines. They were certain to be playing "Rhapsody in Blue," and he'd get to hear a very long segment of the piece before anyone picked up.

Once you get that person on the line, you are subject to the downside of outsourcing; in other words, you're lucky if the person trying to help you can speak English. If he or she can (count your blessings), the corporate system will start to show through. This means the person will be trained in responding to your concern—whatever it may be—with a series of scripted lines that are meant to placate you but are more likely to raise your blood pressure, since they are often delivered in a monotone that makes you question not only the company's commitment to customer service but also the service personnel's ability to read.

All of this would be unfortunate, but not necessarily harmful to the business, if the person assigned to help consumers were actually trained to do so. Too often the problem is beyond the abilities of the person on the phone line, and too often the personnel could not care less. There's not so much as an "I'm sorry"; there is only the disheartening information that you'll have to solve your problem yourself, and we don't especially care how it comes out. Don't call us, and we won't call you.

But that's not the way things have to be. It's a simple formula of promises made vs. promises kept.

If you promise A, B, and C, but deliver only A and B, your customer base will be disappointed. But if you promise only A, and deliver A and B, your customer base will be delighted at how you exceeded their expectations.

In some ways, it's easy to fix a broken window once you've discovered it. You can see it, you can diagnose it, and you can devise a plan to repair it. It might not be easy to make the repair, but that doesn't mean it can't be done. At that point, it's a question of motivation and effort.

The *real* trick is to *prevent* broken windows. It's harder to do, but more rewarding when done properly. Obviously, doing so means the problem that could have arisen will not, and thus the consuming public has an image of your company that is free of faults, or at least the faults that could have been.

Pairing expectation with reality, and then exceeding the expectation, is a wonderful way to avoid broken windows. Analyze your business, determine what the average customer would expect from it, and then give that customer more. There will be very few cases in which this will be seen as negative.

Above and Beyond

In the military, personnel are awarded citations and decorations (and sometimes promotions) for actions "above and beyond the call of duty." This same principle can be applied to your business. Let your employees know that they will be rewarded for effort that goes beyond what most would consider to be the norm. Encourage them to suggest ideas that can improve service or operations. Make sure the right person gets the credit, and promote from within those who do so on a consistent basis.

Remember that a broken window can happen only when someone isn't paying attention—but it doesn't have to be someone who isn't paying attention to his or her job. If the person who works behind the counter at the Dairy Queen is doing a splendid job of serving customers and making sundaes, but also notices that the paint on the ceiling is peeling or that the store is overordering on vanilla and doesn't have enough chocolate, that's "above and beyond."

It's not a question of rewarding someone for being a tattletale—you're not asking your employees to inform on each other. If the counter help mentions the ordering on one flavor or another, this is not an opportunity to chastise the person who is in charge of ordering. It's an opportunity to praise the person who noticed something that can help the company in general.

Having a policy of being considerate and polite to customers is essential, but it's not enough. Those employees who go out of their way to help customers with a problem, who notice the "regulars" and remember their preferences, but are just as accommodating and helpful to newcomers, are the ones who are going above and beyond. But it should be made clear that you expect *all* your employees to go above and beyond, that this is a *company* policy, not an individual initiative. Set standards and then ask the employees for suggestions on how to exceed them.

Ask yourself these questions about expectations and reality:

1. What does my customer have a right to expect when he or she contacts my business?
2. Am I currently providing what my customer should logically expect?
3. Is it being provided by every employee, even the ones who don't come into contact with the public?
4. Are there ways I can *exceed* my customers' expectations for my business?
5. How can I implement these "above and beyond" provisions and remain profitable?
6. Are my employees motivated to find ways to exceed

our customers' expectations? Am I encouraging them to do so?

7. What should I do to go beyond the norm and make my business stand out in the customer service area?

Once you have asked those questions, the answers should tell you a good deal about your dedication, commitment, and procedure. Consider these answers:

What does my customer have a right to expect when he or she contacts my business?

Obviously, this varies from business to business, but there are some constants in all aspects of a customer-oriented business plan. Everyone who contacts any business deserves to be treated with respect and courtesy, to be spoken to as an intelligent human being, to be served as promptly as is physically possible, and to be sure that the person serving his or her needs is dedicated to the same goal as the customer. If the customer has a problem, the employee serving that customer must consider it *his* problem until it is successfully solved.

Am I currently providing what my customer should logically expect?

This can be answered best with the implementation of a mystery shopper. A person who walks into the business unrecognized, presents himself or herself as a customer, goes through every aspect of customer service, and then reports in detail on the experience can be invaluable to the successful business. It's no good if the employees know that someone will be judging them and reporting back—

they will only engage in atypical behavior that will not give you an accurate picture of your operation. Once you know what your business is providing, you can fix broken windows and work on what you *should be* providing.

Is it being provided by every employee, even the ones who don't come into contact with the public?

Often the worst broken windows are people. Employees who do not get the idea of what you're trying to accomplish, who won't "get with the program," who can't push themselves beyond the abysmal standard we have set for ourselves in this society, have no place in a progressive, aggressive business. They need, quite frankly, to shape up or ship out. Get them out before they sink the business.

Are there ways I can *exceed* my customers' expectations for my business?

There had better be. If you're not doing everything you possibly can to make the customer's experience as satisfying and rewarding as it can be, you're not doing all you should do. And there are very few businesses indeed that are doing all they can do. It's a whisker shy of impossible. So think outside the box and consider what you can do that your competitors and others in related industries are not doing, and if it has a benefit to the customers you serve, try it. In most cases, you'll find that customers will react favorably.

How can I implement these "above and beyond" provisions and remain profitable?

In most cases, there is very little or no cost in doing things the right way and getting noticed for it. How much does it cost for each employee to smile? How much does it cost for an employee to take a sense of responsibility for each problem he or she is presented? If an employee can't smile, even for minimum wage, you have the wrong employee, period.

Are my employees motivated to find ways to exceed our customers' expectations?

The mystery shopper can tell you if your employees are doing what you hope they will do—going above and beyond the call. Motivation is another story. Do the employees see a reward in doing things the right way? Are they being recognized for their extra effort (and I don't just mean an Employee of the Month plaque on the wall)?

Am I encouraging them to do so?

Make yourself visible to the employees. Make sure they know that this is a company plan, something that comes from the top and stops at every level down to the person who empties the wastebaskets. It's imperative that your employees understand the benefits of exceeding expectations, and why you expect it to work.

What should I do to go beyond the norm and make my business stand out in the customer service area?

You, as the employer, set the example. If you own a small business, you probably have some contact with the customers yourself. *You* must go above and beyond in order for your employees to understand the importance of the concept. If you are an executive in a larger company, you might not have the kind of contact you once did with the end user. You have to use mystery shoppers and occasionally go to the sales floor or the customer service area yourself. See what's going on and formulate strategies.

Ask your employees for suggestions, but don't rely on them to the exclusion of your own ideas. Be innovative, creative, and open to ideas. Only then can you exceed the expectations that anyone walking into your business might logically have.

WHAT IS REALITY?

- When a customer enters a business, he or she has an *expectation*. How that expectation measures up against the *reality* of the experience will determine how satisfied the customer feels when he or she leaves, and could determine whether the customer will patronize this business again.

- If a business wants to avoid broken windows, its goal must not be to meet expectations for its customers, but to exceed them.

- The customer might not always be right, but he certainly always *believes* he is, and arguing with him will not alter this perception. The two most important words in the broken windows lexicon have to be "I'm sorry." They will be followed closely by "How can I help?"

- If you offer consumers A, B, and C, but deliver only A and B, the consumer will be frustrated and disappointed and will probably not recommend your business. If, however, you offer only A, and then deliver A and B, the customer's expectation is exceeded, and his/her perception of your company will be a much more positive one.

- Employees who go above and beyond the call of duty are the ones who will spot and repair broken windows. Motivating employees to do so is one of the most important jobs a manager has.

Chapter Six

Branding and Broken Windows

Branding no longer refers only to a process that identifies cattle as property of one rancher or another. Today the word also has a much deeper and more vital definition: Branding is the process, the craft, and the art of defining a business in the minds and hearts of the consuming public.

To create a personality for a business, and to have that personality permeate every aspect of the business, to have it *become* the business in the minds of customers, is the goal of branding. It's one thing to have a product, like a plastic coat hanger or a roll of paper towels. It's quite something else to be a *brand*, like Coca-Cola or Sony.

In order to become a brand, to inspire the kind of trust and identification that makes a brand in the consumer's mind, a number of factors must be addressed. Of course, the product or service that makes up the brand must deliver what it promises. It must establish a personality the public finds agreeable and dependable. It must distinguish itself from its competition in some way—by being unique, by aiming at a particular market segment, or by being more attractive to the public than the competition's products or services.

But all these things are tied to a larger concept: the idea of trust. For consumers to accept a brand, to have an opinion—preferably a favorable one—about the brand, and to embrace it to the point that the mention of the brand name is enough to evoke a positive image in the mind, it must *never disappoint*.

In other words, there must be no broken windows.

There is nothing worse for business than to disappoint the customer. In the preceding chapter, I discussed the concept of exceeding expectations. Disappointment, by definition, is the act of falling short of expectations, and that is as bad as it gets for a business. If you don't exceed expectations, you run the risk that the customer will abandon your company for the competition. But if you disappoint the customer, you guarantee that will happen.

When one of the world's most established brands (if not *the* most established), Coca-Cola, decided in the 1980s to abandon its core product and replace it with a drink it called New Coke, the company grossly underestimated the response it would get from its core consumers. Not only did the public not warm up to the new product, it resented the company's elimination of the old favorite, and the fallout from soda drinkers worldwide was devastating. Coca-Cola was forced to reverse gears in a hurry, bring back its old standby as "Coke Classic," and try to convince the public, millions at a time, that it was just kidding.

Try finding a can of New Coke on the shelves today.

This plan was a broken window of epic proportions. It wasn't a tiny thing gone wrong—it was an enormous, elephantine thing gone hideously wrong, a disaster that made the *Titanic* look like a rowboat with a leaky hull. It was a miscalculation that seemed impossible—how could a company not know its consumers well enough to predict that they'd be upset when the product they'd come to know and love for decades was suddenly removed and replaced with something that was closer to—dare I say it?—Pepsi, the drink detested by hard-core Coke fans?

There are, of course, conspiracy theorists who believe the move was a calculated gamble on Coke's part, to create a public relations uproar, a demand for its product so strong it would prove how popular and beloved Coca-Cola was, and to generate goodwill when the original product was resurrected. But it seems extremely unlikely that a company so large, so pervasive, so all-encompassing, would willingly jeopardize its multibillion-dollar prize formula on a hunch. Maybe it always was the plan to bring back "classic" Coke, but I'm willing to bet that the company had much higher hopes for New Coke that never came true. Believe me, they didn't make money on this deal.

The broken window that was New Coke represented more than a wrong guess on the part of some executives. It was a branding catastrophe. When a company goes out of its way to demean its own standing in the marketplace, to take its own core product and say, in essence, that it wasn't good enough and should therefore be eliminated, millions of consumers are going to take that *personally*. They had invested years of loyalty to a product, had in fact been encouraged by the company's advertising to identify themselves as "Coke people" rather than the "Pepsi Generation." The term "cola wars" came to its highest point during the New Coke debacle, given the fact that there were so many consumers who were so angry all at once. It was a golden opportunity for the competition, and one that had been handed to them on a silver platter by a business that was supposed to be one of the smartest in the world. This was a broken plate-glass window the size of the Grand Canyon.

Branding is a process that encourages consumers to identify with a product and to have a positive emotional response to the product. That is exactly what branding theory is about. If you feel good about buying Michelin tires because the animated man made out of rubber is a friendly character who is looking out for your safety, you have willingly given in to the brand's marketing. If you believe that Chrysler cars are made for a different driver than those marketed by Toyota, and you can say clearly which consumer would drive which car, and why, you have been affected by branding.

A broken window that affects the reputation of the entire brand can ruin a business more quickly than a broken window in one franchise, one outlet, or one product. A quick (and entirely hypothetical) example: You walk into a Dairy Queen and see that the counter has not been washed. Your immediate thought is that the crew *at this Dairy Queen* is not performing as well as it should. (Granted, if this is your first visit to a Dairy Queen, you might condemn the whole company for the one store, and if you had seen it consistently in outlet after outlet, you would be right to assume there was a problem with the parent company's policies and switch to another ice cream store, like Baskin-Robbins or Carvel.) If, however, you hear on the news that 130 people across the country have been stricken ill and that the only common trait they have is that they all had Dairy Queen ice cream before getting sick, your perception of the entire chain is now damaged, perhaps irreparably. It will be quite some time, and take a huge effort by the company, before you will set foot in a Dairy Queen again.

This illustrates the danger of a branding broken window. Annoy a consumer in an isolated incident, and you have deteriorated his trust. Break a window on a brand level, and you have made an enemy for life.

What is a brand broken window?

Anything that deteriorates the consumer's impression of the company as a whole, anything that makes the customer or the potential customer think less of the company, is a brand broken window. It's the difference between a mistake that will reflect on one part of the company—a worn rug in one office, for example—and one that will reflect on the company as a whole, for instance, a revelation that the company has been employing sweatshop employees to create its products.

But the implications of a brand broken window go much further than simply a black mark on the company name. It is an emotional response when the public takes a brand to its bosom, and an emotional bond is formed. People can be absolutely passionate about their choice of vehicle, soft drink, basketball team, or coffee. Yes, they "vote" by spending their money on those products, but they also open themselves up just a tiny bit emotionally. They commit to that brand, and not others, because there is something about the product *and the way it identifies itself* that strikes a chord in their sensibilities.

Try to get a Coca-Cola drinker to switch to Pepsi. Talk to a New York Yankee fan about rooting for the Boston Red Sox. Ask the user of an Apple Macintosh what he thinks about Microsoft Windows.

Then you'd better stand back. Fast.

People believe that American Airlines provides a different travel experience than Continental Airlines. Is there that much difference on the flight? Not really; you still get from New York to Los Angeles in five and a half hours or so. You still get a bag of pretzels and a soft drink for free. You still have to stuff your feet and a carry-on bag under the seat in front of you if you're in coach.

But there are differences, and they are the little things that cause a person to choose one airline over another. Let's say one offers a frequent-flier program that allows for a free flight sooner. One brings the drink cart through twice, not once, during a transcontinental flight. One gives you the headphones for the movie for free, and the other charges four dollars. If the fare is roughly the same, which airline are you going to choose?

The devil may be in the details, but the road to success is paved through them as well. Do the small things right—in other words, avoid broken windows—and you can attract a whole new group of consumers who might not have tried your business before.

Now, once you have established yourself in an area, consider how the consumer will react. Your business has worked hard and long, and spent a good deal of money, establishing a brand personality. For an airline, it can be a guarantee of on-time service for business travelers, or an emphasis on comfort. It can have something to do with accommodating families traveling for pleasure. It can be centered on being the lowest-cost airline that still caters to its customers.

Whatever that personality might be, it has to be consistent. After American Airlines came within an eyelash of bankruptcy in 2003, the new CEO, Gerard Arpey, announced that the company would reverse its advertised policy of having more legroom in coach and that it would add more seats so the flights would be more profitable. This may have pleased Wall Street, but consumers (even business travelers) who were choosing American's flights based on the extra comfort were surely not as enthralled. American chose to explain by saying that adding the seats made the flights less expensive.

It doesn't seem like a big thing, a few extra inches of space. I'm six foot two, and I'd rather drink hemlock than fly in a coach seat. But anyone who has ever traveled across the country with cramped legs will tell you just how much those few inches can mean. And the brand reversal—the redefinition of American from the airline that gives you more room to the airline that is taking the room back so your flight can be cheaper—represented an emotional betrayal for some American customers.

When a brand tries to reposition itself, it runs the risk of alienating the core consumers who chose it for what it was to begin with. The slogan "It's not your father's Oldsmobile" was a blatant declaration that the General Motors brand no longer wanted to be associated with the aging clientele it had established, and instead wanted to be seen as young and hip. The strategy didn't work (for one thing, it still *was* your father's Oldsmobile), and the loyal Olds customers were offended by being identified as old and obsolete. Eventually, Oldsmobile was phased out.

Can little things turn a consumer against an entire brand? Certainly, they can. A customer who sees a cockroach at the donut store, for example, might very well stop patronizing every outlet in that chain. The "weakest link" theory is at work here, and it is very strong.

I recently sat with a group of fourteen- to sixteen-year-old girls at a fast food chain called In-and-Out Burger, which operates on the West Coast. Here the core audience for a fast food chain told me they preferred the smaller, lesser-known In-and-Out to a larger chain like McDonald's or Burger King, and it was because In-and-Out paid attention to details.

The bathrooms at In-and-Out weren't as swank as those in a Manhattan hotel, but they were clean, the girls said. The ones at other chains "I try to avoid," one told me. The help at In-and-Out was accommodating and friendly, where others were slow and surly, the girls thought.

Aside from families with young children, teenagers make up the most significant demographic for the "rapid service" industry. And here was a group of teens saying that the little things that weren't done—the broken windows—would turn them away from one chain and toward another.

When a broken window leads to an acceptance or rejection of the brand as a whole, it has transcended its initial role and become a brand broken window. When that happens, it can lead to more than a customer having a complaint for the manager; it becomes something that can alienate the customer from the entire brand, no matter where it is found, forever. And that can't be acceptable to any business, anywhere, ever.

So what can you do? You insist on employees knowing that details are important to the company as a whole, and you enforce the rules. You make sure the rules—whatever your business might be—are enforced throughout the business, in every outlet, by every employee, all the time. In short, you have a burning, maniacal, raging obsession about the details that will set you apart from your competition. And you employ mystery shoppers (best made up of previously disgruntled customers who have registered complaints) to constantly check that the details are being attended to and the broken windows are being avoided or repaired immediately.

You can't allow a broken window to reflect on your brand, or the integrity of your brand and its image will be seriously jeopardized. If you think this is not an important issue, consider two words:

New Coke.

BRAND, NOT BLAND

- To transcend the idea of a product identity and move into the upper reaches of business, it is necessary to establish a brand. And the only way to become a brand in the eyes of the consuming public is to establish trust. There is no other way. None.

- When a company betrays the trust of its customers (think New Coke), it runs the risk of outright revolt and the possibility that its most loyal consumers could very soon be using their wallets to vote for the other side.

- Consumers identify with the brand identity established by the company. It's an emotional attachment, and when it is broken, it is extremely difficult to repair.

- When a consumer has a bad experience with a brand in any outlet, it reflects on every single outlet in the chain. One broken window in one store will become a broken window in every store for the consumer.

Chapter Seven

The Employee as Broken Window

Often the worst broken windows are people.

Yes, I know I've said this before, but it bears repeating. When an employee—any employee—becomes a detriment to the company, for any reason, that employee has become a broken window, and the ripple effect from his or her failure, however slight, can be devastating to your business.

Your employees are human beings, and as such, they are given to human frailty. They will make mistakes, and those are not broken windows. Employees who learn from their mistakes, who become better at their jobs because of those errors, are the best possible workers you can employ. I'm not saying you should fire every employee of your company who has ever made a mistake, because you would have to begin with yourself.

However, there is a significant tendency in business today to forgive more than is rational. We understand why someone is not producing as well as that employee should, we see the problem, and we explain it to that employee. The employee nods and promises to do better. The problem? That employee *doesn't* improve—he or she continues to make the *same* mistakes, have the *same* bad attitude, display the *same* ineptitude or indifference toward the consumers who use the business. And no matter how devastating emotionally it might be for the manager who oversees that employee, there is only one way to make sure that problem won't recur—the employee must go.

The Los Angeles city government employs 37,000 people. In a fifteen-month period in 2003 and 2004, it fired only six workers for doing a poor job. Instead, the system institutes what some people call the Dance of the Lemons, moving incompetent workers from one job to another, losing none of them. This Lemon Dance perpetuates the problem—in fact, compounds the problem—because it guarantees that the worst workers will work in multiple departments. Because laws, civil service regulations, and city ordinances protect incompetent workers, the city doesn't get the service it needs from its employees, who can't be fired. This is about as ridiculous a situation as you could imagine, but it's far from an isolated case.

I'm not advocating cruelty, and I'm not suggesting that you don't treat your employees like people. But continued, persistent bad performance can't be tolerated if you're going to have the intense, obsessive dedication necessary from every employee in order to have success in any business.

The context is irrelevant: What's important is that employees are not so much as admonished for their behavior, which certainly alienates at least one longtime customer and probably irritates considerably more than one. It is an example of the lax, laissez-faire attitude that has infected American businesses in the area of customer service. And the vast majority of such offenses can be traced to employees who have not been given a reason to care.

The concept of training for employees is far from revolutionary. This has been going on since there has been business, starting with the apprentice system and moving on from there (Donald Trump notwithstanding). But the concept of training employees to actually serve customers in a fashion that has all but gone out of style—with courtesy, a helpful attitude, and a smile—has sadly become revolutionary in today's business climate.

A lot of large businesses will tell you (through their publicists) that they work hard and long on employee training. They'll point to concepts worked out by experts in motivation and customer service and how each of these concepts is posted on the wall of every outlet the company owns. McDonald's loves to tell you about its dedication to cleanliness and speed. How clean and fast is the McDonald's you frequent?

The whole concept of employee training in almost every business needs to be overhauled, and here are the concepts that need to be stressed:

1. Customer service
2. Customer service
3. Customer service
4. Employee motivation

5. Advancement for excellent performance
6. Punishment for poor performance
7. See 1, 2, and 3.

Customer service is more important than anything else your business does. It separates loyal customers from ex-customers, and it guarantees a steady stream of revenue for the life of the business. Sales are extremely important, but if customers who buy the product because it's what they want find that the system behind it doesn't for one moment regard them as important, they will look elsewhere. Customer service has to go beyond what is considered good, and enter the "unbelievably accommodating" area. No customer must be allowed to leave a customer service encounter unsatisfied, and that doesn't mean not solving the problem and then asking, "Is there anything else I can do for you today?"

Customer service, in other words, has to far exceed the customer's expectations. It has to be a pleasant experience, not merely an acceptable one, for the consumer. It has to be handled with utmost delicacy, especially with those customers who are, let's say, a little more demanding than others.

How does customer service recover from the abysmal condition it finds itself in today? **Employee motivation.** Employees, even those on minimum wage, can no longer be allowed to sleepwalk through a day's work when dealing with the clientele. They can't be "putting in their time" at work and failing to uphold the integrity of the company with each and every encounter they have. They can no longer be allowed to consider their jobs a distraction from their "real lives." When you're at work, this *is* your real life.

Advancement should be stressed. Employees should know—not just from the corporate statements but through examples they can see in their own outlets—that excellent performance will be rewarded with advancement in responsibility and salary. They should know that those who put in extra effort (and extra effort can no longer be considered smiling and greeting the customer, because those should be the *minimum* standards for encountering a customer) will be noticed and rewarded. They should also know that **punishment** will be the result of poor performance (which in this case will be defined as anything except excellent performance) and that, after the proper number of warnings, they will be terminated.

Businesses these days are far too slow to fire people. Yes, you read that right. More employees should be getting fired. Often they should be fired immediately. Why? Because they are not adequately performing the jobs for which they were hired in the first place. They are coasting, doing their time, merely existing in the company, and not showing the enthusiasm and dedication necessary for making a business run successfully. And I mean every employee, from the newest hire on the counter to the CEO him/herself. Everyone must be accountable, and the person to whom they are all accountable is the customer. There is no higher authority.

Look what happened in corporate America when the customer and the stockholder were considered to be far less important than the people running the company: We got Enron, Adelphia, and WorldCom. Greed overtook good sense, and there was no one at the switch. Even in the largest corporations in the country, when the goal is forgotten, the consequences are as dire as they can be.

In other words, more people should have been fired. *Someone* should have been watching, evaluating the activities of those in charge. On a less criminal (but no less serious) scale, broken windows like poor customer service or slowly declining physical plant—chipped paint, worn carpets—must be someone's responsibility, and that someone needs to be accountable. Fix it or face the consequences.

Jack Welch, the amazing executive who ran General Electric, said that managers who felt they were doing an employee a favor by being lenient were actually doing the exact opposite. They were creating an atmosphere where the employee could do a poor job and feel he was doing an excellent one, and then, when the ax inevitably fell, the employee would not only be unemployed but amazed that such a thing could happen to him. Excuses like problems at home are legitimate, but they can't be allowed to become chronic excuses for poor performance.

The first time a salesperson fails to make his or her sales quota for the month, there must be a warning and an explanation. The second time it happens, if the explanation remains the same and it is not attributable to general conditions in the marketplace that are unquestionably out of the employee's control, that employee must be told in no uncertain terms that the next poor performance will be grounds for termination. Three strikes, and you're out.

But it can get worse. If the worst broken windows are people, consider this: An employee who is a broken window often becomes a virus.

Remember the original premise of the broken windows

theory: that seemingly insignificant crimes left unanswered (fare jumping, graffiti, panhandling) will lead to the impression that no one cares here and that therefore any infraction will be tolerated. Take that idea and apply it to an ineffective, indifferent, or downright bad employee. Left unchecked, that worker will demonstrate to the rest of your staff that poor behavior and an inability (or unwillingness) to perform one's job to the best of one's abilities will be tolerated, even accepted. Silence is agreement. And that will lead the others to emulate the bad employee, and not the example that other, more dedicated workers— including the upper management—might be offering.

A virus spreads through contact with an infected person (in many cases; some are airborne). A broken windows virus starts as an employee who doesn't "get with the program" and is not sufficiently disciplined immediately. Every day that goes by with that employee running visibly counter to the stated policy of the company allows the virus to spread farther and wider throughout your company— what incentive does a worker have to produce when those who do nothing are being rewarded in exactly the same way as those who put in maximum effort?

If the paint department at the home improvement store shows a lack of concern about the customers' needs, it could spread to the flooring department, the cashiers, or the electrical supply—or all three, and more. People tend to emulate what they see, particularly when they are new to a situation, so freshly hired employees will take a look at the existing situation when they begin, and rise or sink to the level of the employees they see in place.

Can you see where this is going? The fact is, there is no excuse whatsoever for letting a poorly performing employee stay on the job. None. If you hire someone with good intentions, and that employee is trying his or her best but can't harness the skills necessary for the job, you have two choices: find another job for this person that better suits his/her skill level or fire that employee. There is no third choice.

If the employee is simply not trying hard enough, or doesn't care enough, to do the job properly, you have to let him or her go. There is, in this case, no second choice.

Jack Welch, arguably the greatest CEO of this generation, addressed the concept of "false kindness," something that I believe too many companies practice regularly. Welch said that companies see their employees as individuals, which is admirable. It's when those individuals start taking on more importance than the company itself that they become broken windows.

If a store manager feels kindly toward a cashier despite that employee's inability or unwillingness to perform her job properly—perhaps because of health problems or trouble at home—the manager might be inclined to let the poor performance slide for a time. That's fine, if a warning is issued in no uncertain terms: "I understand your problem, and I'll do whatever I can to help, but your performance must improve or you will be let go."

And here's the tricky part: *That manager must mean every word he or she says.*

There can't be any hollow promises made here. If that employee does not improve her work, she must be let go *no matter what her personal problem might be.* The company employs many people, and its performance in the marketplace will affect all their lives. Letting one person dictate the fate of the company is not acceptable, and if that sounds like hyperbole, think about it: The other employees don't necessarily know about their colleague's personal problem. They see only the performance, which may be lackluster or downright negligent. And if they see nothing done to undo this problem, *they will assume it's all right with management to behave that way.*

That employee has become a broken windows virus. And it will spread.

Symptoms of a Broken Windows Virus

- The patient (your business) begins to feel sluggish and tired (revenues decline almost imperceptibly at first).
- The patient complains of localized pain (certain departments seem to experience inexplicable slowdowns, due to employee indifference as a learned behavior).
- Family members (other employees) exhibit symptoms (one employee sees another slacking off and emulates that behavior).
- Nonfamily members ask about the patient's health (customers notice the poor customer service and complain).
- Diagnosis is difficult to pinpoint (management doesn't notice the problem and the window is not fixed—the employee is not reprimanded or let go because of poor performance).
- Patient's condition declines more rapidly (as reputation of poor service grows, sales decline and customers find alternative sources for product or services offered by the company).
- Extraordinary measures are implemented (no longer able to deny a problem, management closes retail out-

lets, lays off a percentage of the workforce, and asks creditors for more time to repay debts).

- Patient is put on life support (company files for Chapter 11 protection).
- Patient dies (company goes out of business).

In customer service, the stakes are even higher. One dissatisfied customer is a cancer on the business—they talk to people, they make noise, and they are likely to sway opinions of those who otherwise wouldn't have thought negatively about the company. *Two* disgruntled customers are a full-fledged emergency; they will poison the market. *Three*, and you have a disaster on your hands. Now the entire community thinks of your company as inept, indifferent, or incompetent.

You can't afford that kind of scenario. Your employees must always smile, must always be gracious, must always solve the customer's problem. There is no excuse for anything else. And there's more: Not only must the problem be solved, but the customer has to feel that the problem was the *employee's* problem for the time that the employee was seeing to it. There must be a sense of a common goal, and the goal is always a satisfied customer.

At a coffee bar I once patronized (I feel obligated to note that it was not a Starbucks), a woman working behind the counter told me in no uncertain terms that "smiling is not in my job description." Wow! Imagine that. Nothing can be more basic, more elemental, to customer service than a smile, and this employee felt it was above and beyond the call of duty for her—in fact, was unreasonable to expect of her. A *smile*!

The manager of that store should have immediately

apologized, given me a free cup of coffee, and told the employee that the next customer she faced with anything but a friendly smile would be her last. Instead, like most consumers, I shrugged my shoulders, paid for my coffee, and left.

But I didn't go back to that coffee outlet. Not ever. I'm sure that employee isn't working there anymore, but that's not the point. It's my ultimate power as a consumer, to vote with my wallet.

It's inevitable that the attitude being exhibited was noticed by more than just one consumer. It was undoubtedly seen by many more, and at least some of them would have the same reaction I had—to walk out and never return, because there's always competition, and a customer always has the option of going elsewhere.

As a consumer, you should do exactly that. You should patronize only those businesses you think exhibit the attitude and priorities you feel are important. As a business owner, if you're not paying attention to that kind of broken window, the kind that walks in and punches the time clock every morning, you are inviting disaster. Nothing less. And if you are still in business a year after you've read this book, I can only assume you will have taken this chapter to heart. You're not doing your employees a favor by allowing them to ruin your business. Soon, not only will they no longer have a job, but neither will anyone else who works for you. Because your business will have gone bankrupt and shut its doors.

That is not an overstatement. Let bad employees go, or you are putting your business at risk.

BROKEN PEOPLE

- The worst broken windows are sometimes people. That means an employee who is not on board with the needs and expectations of the company's consumers can do immeasurable damage and is a broken window of the most urgent variety.

- Bad service is inexcusable. Bad service, no matter how good the rest of the factors may be, will always sink your business.

- An employee who can't do the job properly should be fired. Not warned, not shifted to another position, not admonished. Fired. Fast. Before another customer can be spoiled.

Chapter Eight

Why Krispy Kreme Is Better Than Dunkin' Donuts (and Vice Versa)

Be honest: If you were blindfolded and given two donuts to taste, one from Krispy Kreme and one from Dunkin' Donuts, could you really tell which was which?

I don't think so.

Here we have two extremely strong brand names, each selling a product that is not much different from the other's. They are marketed in similar, albeit not identical, fashion, their distribution is similar, and they aim to attract roughly the same type of consumer with the same need. Each would seem, on the surface, to be merely a reflection of the other. The same product with two different names.

But the brand loyalty these two companies command is

staggering. Approaching the level of the Coke vs. Pepsi debate, disagreement among consumers about which is better, Krispy Kreme or Dunkin' Donuts, is intense. They are the Boston Red Sox and New York Yankees of pastry.

How is this possible? It happens because the brand identity engendered by each company is so strong that the consumer feels an emotional connection to the product, one that demands a loyalty not usually seen with so common and affordable a product. It happens because the marketers at each company managed to establish in the consuming public's mind the idea that *their* donut, and not the other one, was the friendly, lovable donut. People care about their donut choice in ways that they don't care about their choice of fax machines, bananas, or paper towels.

I can hear you asking: What does this have to do with broken windows? Hang on. I'll show you.

The emotional connection formed between a product or a company and a consumer is the strongest, best possible bond a business can hope to achieve. It establishes a dedicated, loyal customer for a very long time, and if a company can create enough such consumers, it can ensure itself a long, successful run in its business assuming everything is done correctly. That kind of loyalty is the gold standard for business and is exactly what every business in the world should be striving to achieve.

But it is established early on, when the consumer and the business have their first contact, via advertising, reputation (word of mouth), or direct contact, which would be a retail experience or a service provided by the company to the consumer. In other words, the *first impression* made by the business on the consumer is vital in establishing this strong, important link.

Clichés become clichés because they are, for the most part, true: You have only one chance to make a first impression.

If there's a broken window in the way of that first meeting, you are missing out on an enormous opportunity, and doing yourself irreparable damage. The importance can't be overstated.

Joe DiMaggio was quoted as saying that he always played to the best of his ability on any given day, because there was surely someone in the stands who had never seen him play before, and he owed it to that person to "give them my best." Every day. Every time. DiMaggio, it should be noted, is most famous for having a streak of fifty-six games in a row in which he got at least one hit. That record is mentioned often as being one of the least likely to be broken, and it speaks of consistency and dedication. It would not have been possible if DiMaggio hadn't been thinking of that newcomer in the stands who hadn't seen him before. Joe DiMaggio had no broken windows because he had the obsessive, maniacal rage to do his best every single time.

The first time a person encounters your business, you will make an impression, either positive or negative. And quite often the person your customer will first encounter, the one who will *be* your company for the customer on first glance, will be a cashier, a counter employee, or a retail representative. For online or service-based businesses, that person might be the one who answers the phone. The point is, these employees are usually not the first-hired, best paid, or most personally involved members of the company.

But they had better be the most representative.

Of course, some degree of the responsibility in a first impression is going to fall on the quality of the product or service you offer. You can have the friendliest, most hospitable, most helpful staff in the world, but if your widget doesn't do the job, it's going to sour the experience for the customer, no matter what. Broken windows that start with a bad product or a useless, inefficient service have to be repaired from the ground up and can't be tackled after the fact.

Remember the comparison between Krispy Kreme and Dunkin' Donuts. If either one made a product that tasted bad, a donut that simply wasn't what the customer wanted, it wouldn't matter how well the counter help managed to move the customer through quickly and efficiently. The consumer would simply remember that he or she had gone to a donut store and gotten an inferior product, and there would be no return visit.

But our premise—that the products involved here are not all that different from each other—assumes that there must be some other factor involved in the intense loyalty consumers show toward one or the other. If it's not the product, then what could it be?

There are a number of possibilities, but the two most probable are the physical plant the customer sees and the employees with whom the customer interacts. Remember that a dirty bathroom can be a broken window, and a powerful one. If the customer sees peeling paint, worn carpets, and unwiped counters (especially in an establishment that sells food), a warning light will go off in the customer's head. It is not an overstatement to say that if a traveler pulls down the tray table on a flight and sees the ring of a coffee cup left by the previous passenger, he or she is likely to assume that the engine maintenance done by this airline is not efficient. If that doesn't color a person's view of the airline, nothing will.

If you think that tiny signs of wear or dirt in your facility don't constitute a major problem, you haven't been paying attention to this book. Small signs of negligence from the management of any business are signals that the large things aren't being looked after properly, either, and they alert customers that something is very, very wrong.

When asked about the problems they saw at restaurants (including fast food establishments) they called unsatisfactory, consumers more often than not cite dirty bathrooms, messy counters or tables, condiment areas that have not been cleaned, and other cleanliness problems. Yes, people are upset with lackadaisical or surly service, but they are just as worried about the idea that their food is being prepared and served in an unsanitary facility.

The next most likely factor to make a bad first impression is the employee as a broken window. When a customer encounters a bored, disengaged, listless employee who does not even attempt to solve the customer's problem, the customer will consider this type of treatment to be the company's policy and wonder why the company is so indifferent to serving the people who pay its bills. The customer may indeed reconsider his or her choice of this store or service provider.

But at least there's a chance that a repeat customer has had a positive experience with the company at one time or another, too. In fact, it's likely that's the case, since the customer has chosen to patronize the company more than once, and there must be some reason he's made that decision. There must have been something good at some time that this consumer saw in the company's operations or product to bring him back. It's possible you will lose him based on one negative experience, but not necessarily.

When the bad impression is made on the *first* experience with the company, however, it's extremely unlikely the consumer will become a regular customer. In fact, it's better than even money that you'll never see this particular customer again. Ever.

"People want to go places where they feel welcome," says Jason Binn, publisher of such publications as *L.A. Confidential, Gotham,* and *The Hamptons.* "The second that message is broken up, it leaves a bad impression on any level."

Broken windows aren't simply bad experiences in customer service, however. They can be anything that diminishes the experience the consumer rightfully expects on entering the establishment.

So let's get back to our original question: How do Krispy Kreme and Dunkin' Donuts manage to attract such a loyal base of consumers when the products they sell are not easily distinguishable from each other?

Because one is clearly superior, that's how. Which one? The one with which you had a positive experience *first.*

Let's say you're a Dunkin' Donuts fan. You probably tried that brand before you tried Krispy Kreme. And you had a pleasant experience: The donut you bought was what you expected it to be, or better; it was served quickly and in what appeared to be a clean environment; and the staff serving you was, at the very *worst,* efficient.

In that case, all factors being equal, the product probably made the difference for you. You tried it (maybe you loved the coffee you got as well), you liked it, and you stored that information away in your memory under "Places I Enjoy Visiting."

Perhaps you established a habit at Dunkin'. You went every morning, or every week, or whenever you closed a big deal, as a reward. You tried different varieties of the product, and you liked most of them. You watched their ads on TV and found them amusing. Maybe you bought a Dunkin' Donuts coffee mug to further identify yourself as a fan of the chain.

Now you're invested emotionally as a Dunkin' Donuts consumer. Maybe you told friends about the great coffee they have, or maybe you simply bought a dozen donuts for the last office wedding shower and were given a promotional dozen free. Whatever the situation, you now think of yourself as a Dunkin' Donuts consumer.

When Krispy Kreme came to town, you didn't think of it as a threat—that would be carrying the emotional commitment way too far. Perhaps you were curious about this new brand, and you had heard things about it from others. Maybe you decided that one day on the way to work, instead of the usual stop at Dunkin', you'd give Krispy Kreme a shot.

That's what you gave it—a shot. A chance. An attempt to lure you away from your established brand. And you tried the product, and it was just fine. Maybe the store was about the same: clean, fast, not at all a negative experience.

But the experience wasn't especially superior, either. It

was just about the same as what you were used to. If you'd never been to a Dunkin' Donuts in your life, maybe you would now be establishing a new habit, a new emotional commitment to a company or a product.

But you *have* been to Dunkin' Donuts, and you have already established that commitment. There's no reason to change, because nothing here is demonstrably better.

There are two speeds in today's business climate: fast and dead. The consumer who went to Dunkin' Donuts is lost to Krispy Kreme unless it can be demonstrated that the latter brand is in some way better. If it's the same, the consumer will in all likelihood continue with the buying pattern he or she has already established.

You see how important a first impression can be? And how important it is to make one *fast,* before the competition gets there?

(By the way, the above example could easily be just as true with the product names reversed. If you were a Krispy Kreme fan first and then tried Dunkin' Donuts, there's no reason to think you'd change brands midstream now, either.)

The consumer believes that his brand (and by that, I mean the one he has chosen, not one that he owns personally) is better. Why? Because it validates his choice of that brand to begin with—he identifies himself, even to a tiny degree, as a "Pepsi person" or a "Coke person." He will argue to the death the merits of his brand over the other. And he'll be right, because the human experience is a subjective one, and if he decides his brand is better, it *is* better—for him.

When a broken window like a slow server or a dirty counter establishes a bad impression in the consumer's mind, it is too late. The emotional connection has been short-circuited, and it can't be repaired on the first impression. The only thing that can help is the immediate and total acknowledgment that anything negative was the responsibility of the business and the fault of the manager (or whichever employee is visibly in charge) and the offer of a reward: Here's a free donut, a coupon for a coffee, and the promise that this will never ever happen again.

That might work. But it might not. It's probably best not to get to the point where you have to find out.

HOLE IN DONUT: BROKEN WINDOW?

- Customer loyalty is paramount to establishing and maintaining a strong business. It's great to have lots of customers, but if they come in once and never return, you won't be in business very long.

- First impressions can determine the future of the business. The person who first encounters your customers will be the one they'll remember most. You had better be very careful about who that employee is. The wrong one makes a bad first impression, and there will thus be no opportunity for a second impression.

- The first things your customer will encounter are your employees and your physical plant. The ambiance might be planned, but has it been maintained?

- If your new customer is a loyal consumer of the competition and is here merely to sample the experience, keep in mind that an equal experience (something not better than what he or she has become used to) will not break the customer's loyalty to your competitor. The experience you offer must be *better*.

Chapter Nine

Fly the *What* Skies?

David Neeleman founded jetBlue in 2000, based on the idea that a low-cost airline need not be the no-frills, strap-hanging experience that many people remembered from the People Express experiment in the 1970s and '80s. The new airline would offer no distinction in terms of class—in other words, all seats were the same, and all service was the same; there would be no first class or coach. It did not skimp in terms of the entertainment it provided, offering DirecTV satellite service on most flights. Food was limited to snacks, but not the traditional tiny bag of pretzels thrown at travelers on "the majors."

Above all, the broken window of service would be repaired and never allowed to break again. Charting a course between the saccharine smiles and "buh-byes" of the old days and the surly, irritated flight personnel of most major airlines today, jetBlue decided to insist on service that was professional and efficient without being apathetic.

Neeleman was quoted by the *Los Angeles Times Magazine* as saying that his priorities were to find the middle ground and keep costs down while not sacrificing customer service. In other words, he would pay attention to the details.

"We've tried to say, look, we'll get rid of the food because you don't care about it anyway," the paper quoted him as saying. "We'll have some cool snacks instead and we'll be liberal with those. We'll do tray service so you can get up when the seat belt sign is off and not have a flight attendant tell you to sit down because you're blocking the beverage cart. And we'll do it all with a smile, as opposed to with a whip."[1]

That smile was key. Business and leisure travelers were tired of having to deal with flight attendants, ticket agents, and other airline personnel who seemed so unhappy in their jobs that they couldn't bear to move a facial muscle when dealing with the air travel industry's lifeblood, the traveler. Stand-up comics were doing routines on airline food decades before the airlines cut back massively on serving meals on airplanes, but the food was never the main problem: It was a broken window. The *attitude* that allowed unpalatable food to appear on planes and not be corrected was the problem, and here was jetBlue, dealing with it and solving it in a way that made sense to most travelers. The smile was the signal that things on this airline weren't just going to be different—they were going to be *better*.

The experiment worked well enough for jetBlue to

---

1. Michael Walker, "The Thrill Is Gone," *Los Angeles Times Magazine,* December 14, 2003.

expand its service to airports on the East Coast by 2003 and for other airlines to take notice and try to emulate the success. Delta began a division it called Song, and United opened a division it called (for no discernible reason) Ted; both offer lower-priced flights with some cuts in service but a different image. It is too early to know if these divisions will flourish and become the wave of the future.

Part of what makes jetBlue work is that it operates much more inexpensively than major airlines. Its flight attendants are not unionized, so wages and benefits for employees are considerably lower than at United or American or Continental. Work schedules and rules are relaxed, and that means lower operating costs. Also contributing to lower costs are the lack of meal service on flights and the entertainment deal with DirecTV (which means no fees to Hollywood for in-flight movies). The seats are no more comfortable than on other airlines, but that's easier to take when you're spending a fraction of the cost of a ticket.

Alas, jetBlue is not the rule; it is the exception.

There used to be a slogan that United Airlines had the unmitigated nerve to use: "Fly the Friendly Skies of United." This was, one assumes, in response to customer research that indicated frequent customers felt the service they received on the planes flown by United wasn't accommodating or "friendly" enough. United, it has to be said, missed the point.

It's not enough to *tell* people you're friendly. You have to *be* friendly, too. Otherwise, they will notice the lie, and the consequences can be dire.

United Airlines was hit just as hard as the rest of the travel industry by the September 11 attacks on New York and Washington. Its friendliness, or lack thereof, wasn't a factor in that aspect of its decline. But United *has* declined, and badly. In 2004, its application for relief from the government was rejected. No one in the airline business thinks this is a good thing.

But United's woes are far from an isolated case. American Airlines found itself an eyelash from filing for Chapter 11 protection in 2003, and even without the terrorist attacks of 2001, tourists and business travelers were already disgruntled with the handling they received on the country's airlines (and, for the most part, on other countries' airlines as well).

Why? Well, consider the experience of traveling from one place to another—let's say from New York to Los Angeles, a common business and leisure route. The seats are generally uncomfortable for the six-hour trip, the food is hardly worth considering, the restrooms are tiny, cramped, and often dirty. The entertainment is sometimes acceptable, sometimes not. The service is at best neutral, and often surly. Rules that make no sense are quoted and adhered to without question (*why* can't you listen to a Discman while the plane is taxiing down the runway?), and the airlines make their regard for our intelligence clear to us when, no matter where we're going or for how long we'll be in the air, they insist on instructing us on the proper operation of a seat belt.

And that's in first class. Coach is a form of torture that shouldn't be inflicted on prisoners of war.

There are so many broken windows in the airline industry that it's a wonder any plane is ever in the air, let alone the tremendous number of flights constantly crisscrossing the globe.

The fact is that airlines have had it too easy for too long

when it comes to customer service. They know they have us over a barrel—there's no other way to travel across the country in six hours—and so they inflict whatever cruel and unusual punishment they deem necessary upon us, and we take it. We don't have a choice, other than to go to another airline, which isn't going to treat us a heck of a lot better.

Is it a wonder that people looked at the despicable act of terrorism and, even after the fear had subsided, gave a second thought to traveling by plane? *Without* the attacks, air travel was an ordeal, not a pleasure. It was a necessity, not an enjoyable experience. It was, and is, something we do because we have to, not because we want to. If Captain Kirk's molecular transporter were introduced to the market tomorrow, and the cost was three times that of an airline ticket to the same destination, there would be a grand total of perhaps seventeen people flying the ol' friendly skies the day after tomorrow. And most of them would be pilots.

This wasn't always the case. At one time, flying was considered adventurous, even glamorous, by most travelers. The *Los Angeles Times Magazine,* in December 2003, lamented the loss of glamour in flying, noting that "the airlines lost more than $10 billion in 2002 and have cut more than 100,0000 jobs and parked hundreds of planes in the Mojave for lack of passengers. Planes are flying at near capacity partly because there are fewer of them flying. Some analysts estimate . . . that further bankruptcies and liquidations are inevitable."[2]

Indeed, as airlines like United and American flirted with

---

2. *Ibid.*

(and sometimes took advantage of) bankruptcy protection, it became obvious that people, even before the terrorist attacks, weren't as enthusiastic about flying as they had been since the 1960s. Flying was expensive, it was inconvenient (compared to car or train travel), and it was becoming, seemingly more so every day, unpleasant and impersonal.

Why? Because the airlines knew they had travelers over a barrel, and they didn't care how much they showed it. Food service, long a bane of many travelers' existence, got worse instead of better. Airlines spent less per passenger on food, and in the post-9/11 climate, they *charged* customers for the food the passengers didn't like in the first place. Seats actually got smaller. As noted earlier, American Airlines increased the amount of legroom in coach, advertised it to the public, did not see an increase in revenues, and cut the amount of legroom again.

The airlines were clearly indifferent to the public's sensibilities, but worse than that, they were slapping their key customers—business travelers—in the face. Fares climbed as corporations became more cost-conscious. Service in business class resembled coach more than first class, as the seats were not larger, were not leather, and were not fewer. Attitude among airline staff, from the impersonal Web site booking button that replaced the travel agent to the unsmiling distributor of drinks who replaced the overzealous flight attendant of decades past, was not helpful.

Large air carriers are slaves to customer service surveys, so they had to know something was wrong, but they did very little to stop it. After the September 11 tragedy, there was such a wide swing of emphasis toward security that customer service seemed almost frivolous.

But it has been a few years now since security became the most pressing issue in air travel, and airlines still have not gotten the picture. At least the major airlines have not.

How to Fix the Airlines

When jetBlue's star really started to rise, and the airline began expanding to cities like Boston and two airports in New York City, larger airlines took notice, and they fought back.

American and Delta offered special deals to their customers in those cities: They let customers fly from any New York–area airport (including Newark, New Jersey) to select cities twice during the winter of 2004—and then gave them a ticket free to anywhere in the world the airline flew. That was a huge incentive, although there were stringent restrictions on the use of the free ticket that many customers probably didn't realize at the time. This was a broken window waiting to happen, since travelers would be ecstatic at the time of the offer and then resent the company when they tried to capitalize on the deal.

Delta also competed with fierce intensity when jetBlue announced it would offer a few flights between Atlanta and Long Beach, California. Despite the fact that Delta didn't even fly that route, it matched the jetBlue fare of $99 each way (an introductory loss-leader fare) to Los Angeles, Ontario, and Orange County airports in California and sweetened the pot with triple frequent-flyer miles to Delta SkyMiles members, which practically guaranteed that the members flying from Atlanta to California and back would qualify for a free flight through the program. As a result, jetBlue blinked, and left the Atlanta market.

At the same time, Delta was launching Song and United was unveiling Ted, both of which served limited areas with low cost and the same kind of hipper attitude that jetBlue had pioneered.

Is this the way to fix the airline industry?

Well, yes and no. The broken windows in the airline business are perhaps easier to spot than in most other industries. An airplane, after all, is an enclosed environment and one that most people know very well. A flight is, for the passenger, a simple experience and in most cases a relatively dull and uninspiring one. It's a good sign that some airlines are moving (after considerable prodding from jetBlue) toward lower fares and a better overall experience for their customers.

But so far, that attitude and that philosophy have not bled onto the major airlines; they have been limited to smaller companies-within-companies, and never extended to an entire service area or even the operations in one whole airport, for anyone but jetBlue. United and Delta seem to be giving their customers a choice: Sign up for lower fares in limited runs and get more efficient, friendlier service, or pay full price and get the same miserable experience they'd come to expect.

This hardly seems like a strategy destined for great success. Until the airlines—all of them—are willing to step back, take a look at their windows, and see which are broken, there will be no full-fledged recovery for the air travel industry. The cavalier, callous attitude large airlines have taken with their core customers for decades is now coming home to roost. People fly when they *have* to, not when they *want* to, and they generally shop price, both for family vacations and for business travel.

The lesson taught by jetBlue has been learned by other airlines, but only to a limited extent. In time-honored fashion, they rush to imitate what works without analyzing why it works. Broken windows like airline food, surly service, back-breaking seats, and abominable customer service on the phone are all going unrepaired. Instead, what the public gets is a subindustry of small airlines that want to be jetBlue, but that would prefer to drive jetBlue out of business so they can go back to being Great Big Airlines again and stop with all this customer service nonsense.

The broken windows in the airline industry are not fixed. They are merely taped into place awaiting the next brick to be thrown through them.

The captain has requested you return to your seats and fasten your seat belts. We are experiencing some turbulence.

CARRY-ON LUGGAGE

- All airlines will get you from one airport to another—it's the quality of the experience and the price that will determine a traveler's preference.

- Details like food, entertainment, and comfortable seats make a difference, but indifference and lack of attention are driving the core customer away.

- It is possible to repair broken windows that other companies have missed. By concentrating on details and eliminating what customers didn't like to begin with, jetBlue reinvented the air travel business.

- Imitating success isn't fixing broken windows.

- Only by understanding why the windows were broken can you truly repair them and improve your business. Pretending to fix broken windows by saying you are doing so, and then taking no action, is worse than leaving a broken window unrepaired.

Chapter Ten

Doing It Right

The shining example of the broken windows theory was the spectacular turnaround accomplished in New York City by Mayor Rudolph Giuliani and Police Commissioner William Bratton. While the two, along with others, focused on such broken windows as what Bratton calls "squeegee pests" (men who wash car windshields as a method of begging) and fare jumpers (who leap over turnstiles in subway stations to beat the fare), the murder rate in the city fell from more than 2,200 to fewer than 1,000 per year, and even jaded New Yorkers began to believe their city was more livable than it had been.

Broken windows *can* be repaired, and when they are, the turnaround in public perception is palpable and rapid. But even Bratton himself told me recently that he was "not a believer" in the broken windows theory when it was being developed in the 1970s. It wasn't until later, as a staff lieutenant in Boston, that he saw what he calls "the disconnect."

"I'd go into high-crime neighborhoods and most people did not want to talk about the serious crime," he says. "People were often not aware of the murders, rapes, and robberies because the press was not reporting them. What they were complaining about were the broken windows: What about that abandoned car, what about that prostitute who's on my doorstep every night, what about those kids keeping me up all night? It became apparent to me that we, the police, were focusing too much on too narrow a set of problems, the major crimes. What was causing fear in the neighborhoods was what they were facing every day. In the so-called victimless crimes, the victim was the neighborhood."

What Giuliani, Bratton, and others in New York managed was to shift the focus away from the intangible crimes, the ones that the vast majority of New Yorkers never saw, toward the ones that made their lives less livable—graffiti, panhandling, fare beating. When New Yorkers saw that those seemingly lesser crimes were being handled with an iron fist, their confidence in the police to deal with more serious matters of murder, rape, and assault rose. It was the perception, as well as the reality, in New York City that the broken windows had been repaired.

"In some respects, broken windows was based on what is more common in the business community," Bratton, now the police chief of Los Angeles, says. "Customer service is seen as a broken window. In the police environment, a broken window refers to anything that creates fear or a sense of disorder. It's lack of attention to detail."

When it's done right, repairing broken windows can have a tremendous impact. New York is no longer seen, even after Giuliani's administration is gone, as a haven for crime or a dangerous place. The threat of terrorism, a much more national concern and certainly anything but a broken window, is considerably more palpable in the city today than the fear of crime. Police officers on the street are seen as public servants and heroes, not corrupt individuals unwilling to deal with the problems of average citizens.

What Bratton and Giuliani did in New York was remarkable, but it came down to the fixing of some broken windows. Businesses, as well as governments, can and must do the same.

In some cases, the results of broken window repairs have been staggering.

I referred in the preceding chapter to the success of jetBlue, the airline that lowered fares while increasing customer service. It has to be noted that by avoiding broken windows, jetBlue managed to create an image of itself as the people's airline, the one looking out for the traveler, and not merely its own bottom line. It even ran an ad in which everyone at the airport got along famously—right down to the dogs and cats. "Is it always like this around here?" someone asks. "Only when the jetBlue flights arrive," another answers.

That's the kind of good feeling the airline aims to create for its customers. And based on the ticket sales and revenues, it has to be concluded that jetBlue is succeeding.

It's easy to point a finger when windows are broken, especially when those broken windows are left unrepaired for long periods of time. It's easy to assume the company doesn't care—and in some cases, that assumption would be correct. Broken Windows Hubris isn't an isolated disease; it affects many large corporations whose executives think they are more important than the satisfaction of the company's customers. It happens quite a bit in business, and in each case, it is deplorable and inexcusable. But it is easy to find and point out.

Much more unusual is the company whose broken windows are noticed, identified, and repaired promptly, so as to best serve the customer base and keep the company's mission alive and well. There are some, and they deserve a good deal of attention.

Target Stores

Where Kmart stumbled and Wal-Mart ran into problems, Target quietly became perhaps the most respected and trusted name in the mass merchandise market—no small feat for any company, let alone one that was hardly well known as little as ten years ago.

The concept with Target was always clear, and its windows remained gloriously unbroken. Yes, there would be plenty of merchandise on the shelves, and yes, the prices would be competitive, if not guaranteed to be the lowest. But Target concentrated on establishing its identity as the mass merchant whose stores were designed with the *customer* in mind, and that made the difference.

Speed was the key: Even consumers whose priority was to find the lowest price on every single article on their shopping list wanted to be in and out of the store quickly. Target made sure that could happen: There would be no long waits on checkout lines. If too many people were on line in one location, another register would immediately be opened, and the wait was decreased. Even during the madness of the holiday season, Target kept its customers moving through the store (and especially the process of paying for merchandise) as quickly as it possibly could.

Was this a simple business practice, designed merely to increase traffic by speeding customers through the store in order to make room for others? Certainly, it was. But it was also an acknowledgment to consumers that the owners of Target had been to large chain stores before, knew what the problems (broken windows) were, and were making an extraordinary effort to avoid them *in order to make the shopping experience easier and more pleasant for the customer.*

Even when Target's stores inevitably fall victim to the same broken windows inherent to the mass merchandising industry—less-than-sparkling facilities, underpaid, indifferent help—its mission, to remain competitive with and faster than the rest of the industry, is intact and noticeable. The broken windows it suffers are repaired more quickly than most, and the communication with consumers (some of whose complaints are studied carefully by executives) is better than the rest of the industry. Better than that, Target has stayed off the front page of the news section, with no class-action suits filed against it and no Chapter 11 protection requested. Those broken windows are harder than most others to repair, as they are the result of many other, less noticeable broken windows that must be repaired at the same time.

Target has managed to retain its original concept even while expanding into many new markets, which is usually the critical juncture for a chain of businesses. The larger a chain becomes, the more difficult it is to maintain the obsessive, raging devotion I've described as essential to the discovery and repair of broken windows. So it is especially interesting to watch a business as it goes from one store to two, from two stores to six, from a small chain in one state to a regional chain in three, and then to a nationwide business. At each step along the way, as more control is ceded, it is often easier to see the broken windows accumulate.

Not in Target's case. Here, as the chain moved into every state in the Union and expanded its presence further, the original concept of the stores and the devotion to preventing and fixing broken windows remained evident. This was a case of a business that kept sight of its vision and made sure its windows stayed uncracked.

The Walt Disney Company

Let's forget for a moment that Disney seems to own half the planet. Let's overlook the subsidiary businesses of television networks, retail stores, and clothing manufacturers. Let's examine the core business of the Walt Disney Company: family entertainment and theme parks.

Consider, especially, the experience one has when attending a Disney theme park in Florida, California, or anywhere else around the globe. If ever there was an atmosphere in which no windows are broken, this is it. Cleanliness is famously obsessive; there is never—*never*—

a candy wrapper left on the street. Problems are solved immediately by a staff that is (get ready, it'll be a shock) *cheerful* about doing their jobs, and enthusiastic about making sure the customer's (guest's) priorities are the most important thing. If you have a problem and a Disney "cast member" can't solve it for you, it must be quite a problem, because your enjoyment of the stay in the park is what has been drummed into the head of every employee in that park, and you'd be hard-pressed to find one who doesn't adhere to that philosophy.

Nothing is perfect: No one can regulate the weather, and Disney parks tend to be in areas where the sun shines bright but hot. Lines are unavoidable in a place that has tens of thousands of visitors each day, all of whom want to attend the same attractions and might even have similar schedules in mind. But consider the lengths to which the Disney parks go to accommodate those conditions and make the guest's stay easier and more enjoyable.

A few years ago, a system was installed called Fastpass, which allows guests to reserve a place in line. Guest tickets are swiped in a machine, and a time to return is reserved on a ticket. The guest can then go to any other attraction in the park, come back at the appointed time, and see the attraction without waiting in line. This addressed the most serious broken window in the parks— families having to spend long, hot hours on line for an attraction that would last four minutes.

The solution was simple, yet demonstrated the park's obsession with making the day enjoyable for its customers.

By the same token, Disney's entertainment arms (its film divisions, particularly Walt Disney Pictures, over which the company maintains total control) offer what has to be described as a branded experience. Go to a Disney movie for the family, and you know what you're going to get. Not to worry about the kids dealing with issues or images they may find confusing or frightening; in this case, the experience will be what was intended by the company's founder. Yes, other divisions of the same company will offer more challenging fare, but it will be labeled as such and come out under a different banner.

Disney has its problems, like any other enormous corporation. But its core businesses retain their vision and make sure their windows remain unbroken.

Apple Computer

Scoff if you want to; tell me that Apple controls only 3 or 4 percent of the personal computer market. But then talk to any Apple owner and see if the glint in his eye is maybe a little bit more intense than someone who just bought a Windows system. Ask him if he'd like to change his allegiance in computers. Then stand back, because the response will not be a calm one.

Apple's crowning achievement is in creating obsessed, crazed *consumers*. Its products, innovative as they have been for two decades, are more expensive than IBM-based systems. They don't have access to nearly as much software as those running Microsoft systems. Apple users are, from any rational standpoint, at a considerable disadvantage in today's marketplace.

And yet they are the most devoted consumers on the

planet. They will not change their purchasing alliance in computers under threat of death. They will spend hours explaining to you why 95 percent of the world's computer buyers are wrong and they are right. And they will happily pay those higher prices for that hardware that can't run as many programs as the less expensive ones and will be happy and proud each time they do so.

Now, *that's* loyalty.

How has Apple engendered such devotion? I contend it is through their policy of noticing and repairing broken windows, sometimes before they are broken.

Each of Apple's innovations, from its initial operating system through the introduction of the Macintosh, and then the iMac, computer, has been designed with one thought in mind: making computing easier or more enjoyable for the consumer. Microsoft's Windows system is largely based on the original Macintosh operating system and still lags behind in speed and ease of use. Apple continues to think like a computer user, not like a computer company.

Then there is the issue of customer service. Call Microsoft with a problem sometime and try to get help. I dare you. You'll get endless voice mail prompts, demands for money, and eventually an outsourced computer tech in Pakistan who may or may not solve your problem after charging you for the call.

Call Apple with the same problem. Your warranty will last longer on an Apple computer, so you might not have to pay a dime for help. But you'll get a human being sooner, and unless there's something seriously wrong with your computer, your problem will be solved—and solved by someone whose problem is yours until it is solved—before you get off that phone.

Apple users are considered fanatics. Most businesses would be hard pressed to find such customers; for Apple, they are the rule, not the exception. I think it has something to do with the company's windows.

GETTING IT RIGHT

- Fixing broken windows is like quitting smoking—the sooner you do it, the more completely your problem will heal and reverse itself.

- Broken windows *can* be fixed, and they *can* be detected before causing trouble. The crime situation in New York City is an example in government, while Apple Computer, Disney, and Target are examples in business.

- Simply saying you've fixed the window isn't enough. You have to demonstrate your devotion to customer satisfaction and make sure your customers know it's more than talk.

Chapter Eleven

Do You Google?

There are many successful businesses in the world. Very few of them have become a verb.

Can you "Coca-Cola"? Do you "Sony"? Have you ever "BMW-ed" or "McDonald's-ed"?

But I'll bet that you've Googled. You may have done it today, as a matter of fact. You might have found this book via Googling.

Google, which started out as the Little Search Engine That Could and became a multibillion-dollar public stock offering, does not any longer need to explain its function to any member of the general public. If you tell someone that you Googled them as a way of finding out about their business, they will probably nod in recognition. Before this meeting, they probably Googled you.

Naturally, a semantic change doesn't mean you have a successful business. But the fact that your business name has become recognizable enough that people are using it independently and everyone knows what it means is an indication that you have defined your business well. Few things are as important in business.

But that kind of name recognition, when it's not negative (Enron, anyone?), is also an indication of something else: It means that you have done a good job in fixing your broken windows.

The Internet is an incomparable information-gathering tool, but its windows can be absolutely shattered when things don't go right. A key example of such broken windows had been the very core of the Internet itself: the Web search engine. After all, if you aren't able to find the information available, what good is it to have the information available in the first place? From a business's point of view, the search engine can be much more valuable; having a killer company Web site is of very little use if the public isn't being made aware of its existence. Search engines have come and gone and until recently, were interchangeable, easily confused machines that couldn't really be counted on to perform the task they were designed to undertake.

That changed when Google became synonymous with "search engine." In what seemed like a flash, www.google.com was *the* place to go for data searches, and it provided the same basic service as the rest, only better.

How can something this generic (you ask for information, and you get it) be characterized as better? How can one be a better search engine than another? Is Google really of higher quality than Excite, Yahoo!, AltaVista, Magellan, or Ask Jeeves? Why does a Web site that charges nothing for information (and none of these search engines charge) have to be better?

Google managed to turn itself into the most visible and well-known search engine through its handling of potential, and existent, broken windows. It saw problems with the way some other search engines handled their service, and it avoided them. Even when Google itself had a breakdown of some sort, the focus was kept on service of the user (you can't call someone a customer if the service is free), and the broken window was repaired quickly and efficiently. In many cases, users didn't even notice.

Search engines proliferated wildly in the 1990s. As home and business Internet use increased dramatically through the decade, the need for a "road map through the information superhighway" became clearer. But once people (mostly home users) got over the novelty of the concept—the ability to find almost any piece of information in an instant—the cracks in the windowpanes began to show.

In some cases, search engines that were asked for information wouldn't understand the request. Unless certain words were put in quotation marks, they would be misinterpreted. Capitalization mattered in some cases, but not in others. Keywords were helpful, but they sometimes led to the wrong conclusion. There wasn't anyone to ask for help.

The companies that owned the search engines were also trying to establish their Web sites as "destination sites" for users, so as to increase the probability that larger companies would advertise on the sites, which is the way search engines make money for their owners. It was hard to establish a brand personality, since the product being sold—information—was the same for each search engine, but different for each user attempting to find it.

In short, the only difference among search engines was the broken windows—the number and type of them. The sites with more broken windows (slow service, programs that didn't understand the questions) fell by the wayside, and the familiar names we know now remained.

But Google became a verb.

Somewhat late to the starting gate, Google learned from the experience of those who had preceded it into the search engine parade. Its founders, Sergey Brin and Larry Page, knew that users didn't want to be held up in their search for whatever tidbit of information was the emergency of the moment, so speed—the currency of the Internet—was essential. Google would be fast.

Google also had to be accurate. Here its founders decided to err on the side of excess: If you asked Google for a piece of information, it would bring back every Web site it could find (and it is currently scanning more than 4 billion sites) that had the keywords you requested. Sometimes the list of "hits" would be compressed, but when it was, Google would let you know it had done so for efficiency's sake, and offer to give you the entire list of eligible sites, no matter how ridiculously long it might be.

Still, was that enough to make an impact on the millions of users who thought that one search engine was roughly the same as the next? It took time, but Google began to separate itself from the pack largely through word of mouth, but also through effective marketing. Google became the search engine of choice for other sites offering news and information. "Powered by Google" became the logo most often seen when a related Web site would offer a search engine. The implied message was that if another site thinks enough of Google to use it instead of creating a search engine of its own, Google must be good.

And the fact was, from a user's standpoint, Google *was* good. It was better than other search engines in small ways that made a difference. In short, it had fewer broken windows, and they weren't broken as badly as others.

Google's Road to Success

1. **Google was fast.** Most search engines were, and are, but Google's speed was designed to be especially noticeable—and if you didn't notice it yourself, the elapsed time of the search (0.35 seconds seemed pretty fast) was listed on the first page of your search results.

2. **Google was accurate.** If you searched for a keyword, Google would highlight that word in each result it gave you, to show that you had gotten what you asked for. If you got something else, the highlighted keyword would indicate that maybe the problem was yours. But it could be fixed.

3. **Google was easy to understand.** If you did get inappropriate results, Google had a help button that would clearly explain the procedure and demonstrate how to repair the problem (the broken window on your part?) and get the results you wanted.

4. **Google was thorough.** Other search engines would take your request and give you the top ten results (those most likely to be the site you were seeking) and give you more only if those weren't good enough. Google gave you as many results as it could find, and let you sort through them. Yes, it ranked the

results by the same criteria as the other engines, but it let you decide what was enough.
5. **Google was free.** Okay, so was every other search engine (except for specialized supersites like Lexis-Nexis), but when you're offering improvements on what's available elsewhere, and you're still not charging any more than the competition (or in this case, not charging anything), you're in line to succeed.

Google's success—it came from nowhere and got itself into a position to make its founders multibillionaires—can be attributed mostly to its ability to deal with broken windows. This is key, as Google offers no tangible, physical product. It offers a service and, as such, must serve its consumer base better than its competition to stand out and keep its reputation. The fact that the site is listed as one of the five most often visited every week is an indication that the strategy is working.

This is another example of a company whose founders and chief executives got it right. They knew that windows could not be broken and stay broken in a business that relies on satisfied consumers to be profitable. They knew that little things—an extra second or two of waiting, a few highly placed search results that didn't really match the request—would make a large impression on the people the company could least afford to offend. And they determined that such things would not happen and that the tiniest infraction (broken window) would be alleviated as quickly as was possible.

Google doesn't rely on face-to-face contact with the consumer; that is, the average user is rarely in contact, either in person, by phone, or even online, with another human being who is concerned with his or her situation. Google, as a search engine, is run (from the consumer's viewpoint) by computers. No person could possibly search through 4 billion Web sites in 0.35 seconds.

So customer service for Google is different than for most consumer-based companies. It means the delivery of the promise the company makes without, in almost all cases, direct human contact. It means the product must almost literally speak for itself, and it had better be good, all the time, because users are going to come back to it again and again if it is, and give up after one try if it's not.

Google's staff deals much more intimately with the advertisers who pay their bills, but as long as the product delivers the "eyeballs" the industry tracks in large numbers, those advertisers will be happy to be seen on a site that has a prestigious name. They know that consumers make multiple trips to Google and that they are almost always satisfied in what they have set out to do.

Ask anyone you know if they have Googled, and even if they don't answer affirmatively, they'll know what you mean. But more important than that, they will not have a negative story to tell about the Google experience, and in a service-oriented business, that is not only remarkable, it is absolutely key to success.

The experience of using Google isn't, to be fair, all that different from the experience of using most other major search engines. The variations I discussed above—speed, accuracy, and volume—aren't enormously pronounced, although they are noticeable. Consumers will detect a difference, but it's not like other search engines are awful and Google is impeccable; it's a question of degree.

Still, the difference in *perception* is quite large. People don't talk about "AltaVista-ing" something to find it on the Internet or "Yahoo!-ing" their own name to discover what information about themselves is available to the general public. Google has gone beyond most brand names—and in the minds of consumers, it has gone beyond most services—in reliability and consumer friendliness. Google just has a better place in the public's mind than its competitors.

It has done this essentially without advertising and without making a huge consumer campaign that would define its persona and create an impression in the public's mind. Google has managed this feat chiefly through performance, which is rare in consumer culture and rarer still on the Internet, where almost nothing is what it claims to be.

This should speak to all businesses, not just Web-based ones, on the power of performance and fixing broken windows (or avoiding them altogether). It should be a wake-up call to every business that believes it can create an image with advertising, public relations, and public pronouncements, but not deliver on its core promises. If a business believes it can make charitable contributions and publicize them, but not see to the small details of its own operations, it should look to Google not for inspiration, but for an object lesson in everything Google isn't doing wrong.

Practicality dictates that a business do what it promises to do, and Google does that. But broken windows are often hiding below the surface (in the basement, if you want to carry the metaphor that far), where they aren't easily visible. The fact that a business that almost never comes into direct contact with consumers can establish itself as a worldwide presence and a household name by getting the little things right should speak volumes to anyone who is trying to start or maintain a business in today's climate.

Don't just Google something; think about Google when you do it. There are myriad lessons to be learned here, and most of them are tiny, not easy to see. They require a dedication to observe, but their importance can't possibly be overestimated—they can be the difference between your business's success and its failure.

Does that remind you of anything?

GOOGLE ME THIS, BATMAN!

- Even for a business whose relations with the public are not face-to-face, performance counts. Tiny imperfections in the product or service offered become amplified when there is no human contact with the company.

- When a business is not enormously distinguishable from its competition, the details become even more pronounced and important. Broken windows make the difference when the competition is close to your level. Go a little bit further, and you will be noticeable. Don't, and you're a member of the pack.

- A broken window doesn't have to be a "problem"; it can be merely a service you could offer and don't. If you can do something more for your customers, do it, and you will make a lasting positive impression.

Chapter Twelve

Broken Wires: Broken Windows on the Net

It's one thing to interact with your consuming public in your retail stores, or on the phone when a customer service call is made. It's something else again to interact with the people spending their money on your product or service via your company's Web site or by e-mail.

The Internet is the most perfect, pervasive, and all-encompassing source of information in the world—you can find virtually (pardon the pun) anything you could possibly want to know in a matter of seconds. And as a business, you are able to convey the message you especially want to communicate quickly, without filtering, and inexpensively. It seems a perfect tool.

But the Net is also a minefield of broken windows. When something goes wrong with your Web site, especially if it is not well organized or designed, the public will find it immediately and become increasingly annoyed with your company—and the worst part is, you might not even know there's a problem until it's much too late.

Imagine: A customer buys your product in a traditional, brick-and-mortar retail outlet. He brings it home, opens the packaging, begins to assemble it, and discovers that there is a small piece of hardware—a bolt, let's say—missing.

Let's say that instead of calling customer service personnel on the phone, this consumer decides to go online and visit your Web site to alleviate his problem. There are any number of ways this transaction can become a broken window, and because there are very few scenarios in which the consumer interacts with an actual human being online, it's quite possible you won't be aware of the problem until the customer is already more than irritated and might be a customer of yours no longer.

First, the consumer has to find your Web site. Most companies are savvy enough these days to list their Web address (URL) on all promotional materials and even packaging, so the customer in question here would be able to look on the box or the instruction booklet to find the proper address. It had better be there, or that is a major broken window.

Assuming that the address is found, either on your materials or via a search engine like Google (see the preceding chapter), the consumer will now search your home page for the customer service link. This brings up two distinct, and eminently possible, broken windows: You must have a customer service link on your home page, and it must be easily findable.

A consumer who needs assistance with your product or service is not in a forgiving mood to begin with—he has spent money on something that doesn't seem to be working properly, and he is heading toward frustration. So if the road to the customer's solution runs through the Internet site for your company, it had better lead there directly and quickly. Finding a home page with a badly placed assistance link (or worse, none at all) is just going to add to the customer's sense of irritation. That's not a help; it's a broken window. A *big* broken window.

Let's assume, though, that you've managed to vault those hurdles: Your URL is easily attainable, your home page has a link to customer assistance, and it's easy to find. Now, how does the customer assistance page on your Web site work?

In many cases, customer service on company Web sites is relegated to a section labeled "contact us," and it is merely a link to a general e-mail address the company uses to field customer complaints and comments. But this doesn't give the customer a sense that his problem is being considered or solved quickly; it serves only to make him more anxious and annoyed than he was before. It could be days—weeks!—before his seemingly simple problem is even considered, let alone solved. This is the information superhighway? It feels more like an unpaved road leading to a dead end.

A customer service page should offer exactly that— customer service. A consumer bringing his or her problem to your Web site is in need of answers, solutions, and he or she needs them *now*. When you use a communications system that can send millions of messages in a fraction of a second and your use actually adds time to the problem, that's a broken window.

Yes, there should be a way for a consumer to contact

the company on your Web site, and yes, it can certainly be a direct link to an e-mail generator. But it should also include the company's "snail mail" address and phone number, in case the consumer wants to get in touch the old-fashioned way. And that contact link should not be considered the customer service section of the Web site.

Instead, there should be a separate section for those who have issues that need to be addressed, and it should be comprised of three elements. There should be a "frequently asked questions" (FAQ) link, where the most common, and easily solved, complaints are listed and explained in clear language. There should also be a detailed section for each product the company sells, detailing its operation and answering its FAQs, plus offering order forms for extra parts or accessories.

But most of all, there should be, whenever financially possible, a real-time, live-person customer service feature. This is available from many larger companies' Web sites and ensures that customer service professionals, usually the same ones who answer phones for the company's consumer help lines, are available online to answer questions in an instant message (IM) format, speaking directly to and with the consumer as questions are asked.

Yes, it's expensive, and smaller companies might not be able to afford the luxury. But if you have a staff of people answering customer service calls on the phone, there is no reason not to expand that service to the Internet, since you are already paying the employees, and the overwhelming odds are that all of them have a computer terminal at their workstations.

Here's why it's important: A consumer who is contacting customer service begins with a problem. In almost every case, this is someone who doesn't have a *question* about your product or service, it's someone who has gone ahead and purchased that commodity and is now having trouble using it. It's entirely possible that the problem is of the consumer's making—perhaps he or she doesn't understand (or hasn't read) the instructions or is trying to customize the product in some way for which it wasn't intended. That doesn't matter. The consumer has a problem and needs it to be solved.

When someone chooses to contact customer service (where, you'll recall, we have already established that the bulk of broken windows are broken), he has made a conscious decision not only to seek an answer to the problem at hand but to try to obtain that answer quickly. He could, after all, have returned to the place where he bought the product or service, or written a letter to the company requesting assistance. No. He has opted, instead, to call or go online to get an answer *now*.

The choice of online help, rather than telephone assistance, is a significant one. Remember, the whole idea of personal Internet use is that the information is supposed to be delivered conveniently and quickly. That's the reputation that the Web has, and as Marshall McLuhan noted, the medium is the message. The customer is sending you a message by choosing to contact you through his computer, the fastest communications device yet invented by man.

"You have so many choices, and we have so little to go on to make choices," says Malcolm Gladwell, author of *The Tipping Point* and *Blink,* a man who knows a great deal about why consumers make specific choices. In a recent interview, Gladwell told me that "our decisions come down to relatively subtle things. Our unconscious acts as a filter and then our conscious mind takes over from there. We can reject things on an unconscious level without even realizing we're rejecting them. We gather every available piece of information very quickly and then do a kind of first cut."

Gladwell, whose book *The Tipping Point* was a massive best seller and a brilliant examination of what makes businesses work well or not at all, knows about decision-making, and he knows that the "unconscious filter" extends to the decisions we as consumers make in interacting with companies. Maybe the awful telephone experiences that many consumers have with customer service (the multiple broken windows of phone message systems, long waits on hold, and surly customer service representatives out-sourced in countries where the accents make it difficult to communicate) lead us to opt for online assistance. If so, companies should note that the online customer service experience had better be demonstrably more efficient and pleasant an experience, because the consumer is coming in with a negative expectation, even if it is an unconscious one.

Given that, we have to examine the way in which the average company Web site deals with the public in general, even when they are not coming to the URL with a problem. Because remember, the little things you do, good or bad, send psychic signals to the people with whom you most hope to communicate: your customers.

When someone stumbles across, or seeks out, your home page, what does that person find? If the information there is delivered in a cluttered, disorganized, confusing fashion, what does that tell the visitor about your company? If the most logical, predictable questions about the company—address, phone number, type of business—aren't answered easily, what message does that convey? If the personality projected by the site isn't one that is friendly, helpful, and useful, what message do you expect the visitor to take away from this experience?

It's important that your message and your image be consistent every time you come into contact with the public—and that certainly includes your Web site. As the face of your company on the Internet, this section, which is designed and executed by people who work for your company, must be an absolute paragon of unbroken windows. Here, where you have the most control over your message, every detail must be exactly right. And that means special attention to every possible facet *before* anything is posted and open to exposure to the general public.

But don't make the mistake of promising more than you can deliver. We all know the difference between the TV commercials aired by McDonald's (in which gleaming, smiling young people offer wholesome food in sparkling settings) and the reality of going to a McDonald's outlet (well documented in chapter 2). Making claims on your Web site—even subliminal ones like "cleaning up" images that you can't hope to duplicate in real life—that won't match the customer's experience in a nonvirtual setting is a broken window, and a dangerous one.

"The distance between the beautiful image on the television [commercial] and the reality in the [McDonald's] store is now so great that you've made the [negative] encounter in the store more salient," says Gladwell. "This is not the McDonald's you expected."

By the same token, if a company's Web site offers an

image that is unrealistic and inflated, it will poison the experience the customer can logically expect to have with the company in "real life." So make sure your Web site offers a positive view of your business, but one that is true, or you will be asking for unfavorable comparisons, a seriously broken window.

Make sure everything on the site is easy to understand. People are more sophisticated technologically than they were even a few years ago, but the general public should not be expected to understand even the basics of HTML code. Make it easy for them to point and click their way to the information they need, in as few moves as you can manage. Ease and simplicity of use are enormously important factors in a commercial Web site.

There are a number of reasons a person will seek out your Web site: information about your product or service; information about getting a job with your company; information about contacting your company; information about the history of your company; customer service. In any one of these cases, the information should be simple to find and written in language that is easy to understand. This is not because you're assuming the consumer is an idiot; it's because people want a pleasant, stress-free experience from your Web site, and while you don't have to write everything on a second-grade level, there's no reason to make it any more confusing than it needs to be.

In addition, design is important. Make the site easy to look at, as it will be seen by any number of people, including those who might stumble across it by accident. Don't you want their business?

Broken windows on the Internet can include things you don't have on your site. For example, if a person comes to the home page with the intent of e-mailing a specific person in your company (one who deals with the public, as every employee does not need to be listed), that person's e-mail address, or at least a common address through which that person can be reached, should be listed. If there's no way to find that information on your site, you're increasing the visitor's frustration level, and that is never good for business.

The key is to remember what you yourself find helpful and irritating about your visits to corporate or company Web sites. Use what you think is a positive factor and make sure that the negative ones (the broken windows) are avoided. And test everything before you post it to your site.

When the site is up and running, it's a good idea to mystery shop your Web site as you would your business. Visit every once in a while. Make sure all the links still work. Make sure you can e-mail with a question or complaint and that no new product (or old one) is unrepresented.

If you get only one chance at a first impression, keep in mind that the first time many people encounter your business is online. Do you want to begin with a bad experience?

Web Gems

- A company's Web site is a place where impressions are made and customer service is rendered. It is as important as any aspect of a business in which consumers are directly encountered.

- Simplicity is important, in both design and operation. Make sure the Web site for your company is easy (and hopefully enjoyable) to use.

- Customer service on the Web is important and tricky. If you can't offer twenty-four-hour live help, by all means include e-mail addresses and toll-free phone lines where the answers to consumer questions can be gotten as quickly as possible.

- Don't make Web promises you can't keep. If you include pictures of facilities that are more impressive than your actual ones, you are creating an image for the customer that your business can't live up to.

- Make sure you present the information in clear, concise, easy-to-read formats and offer as much information as you think consumers might need, and then some.

Chapter Thirteen

The Public, Watchdog

My friend Jeffrey Cohen is a New Jersey–based author and freelance writer, but he's also a serious movie buff. Between Jeff and his son, pretty much every studio release is open to discussion. So they go to the movies a *lot*.

One thing that some theater chains have done in the past few years to increase revenues (and keep in mind that studios, not theaters, make most of the money from your ticket purchase on a new film) is to show television-style—and in some cases, actual made-for-television—commercials for products other than upcoming movies. The pre-show, as theater owners call it, the time after the lights go down and before the movie begins, used to be for coming attractions featurettes, or trailers, as they're known in the trade. Now ads for sodas, cars, and clothing, among other products, are being added to the pre-show.

This steams my friend in New Jersey more than I can tell you. "If I want to see TV commercials, I don't have to spend nine dollars to do that," he'll say. "I can stay at home and watch them for free."

So when Jeff discovered there was a chain in his area that didn't include commercials in the pre-show, but retained only the coming attractions trailers, he made sure he and his son patronized that chain whenever possible, which is almost all the time.

But that's not the whole story. Jeff has been telling his friends in the area (and out of the area, like me) about the chain that keeps commercials out of the theater. He's making sure they know, and encouraging them to pay their money—to vote with their wallets—to the theater chain that doesn't show commercials.

Now, by our definition, showing commercials before a movie isn't necessarily a broken window. It doesn't automatically convey to the consumer that the chain isn't paying attention to details or doesn't care about serving the needs of its patrons. But it could be construed as a sign that the business is more interested in improving its bottom line in any way possible than it is in the sensibility of its customers. The movie will be the same in any theater showing it, give or take a decibel or two. Why not patronize the one that keeps an annoying trend out?

Will Jeff and his friends make a huge impact on the theater chains they shun? Probably not so much that the owners would even notice. But if enough people feel the way he does, and notice that there is a place that doesn't show commercials before the movie, that could start a trend. Think Malcolm Gladwell's *The Tipping Point*.

The public is the final arbiter in almost every business. They buy your products, use your services, and pay your bills. In Hollywood, movie stars' careers rise and fall based on the number of people who attend their films. In politics, the numbers are even clearer (most of the time): The candidate with the highest number of votes is the one who gets to have, or keep, the job.

Thinking that you can get by because "they won't notice" is tantamount to putting a noose over your head and jumping off a stepladder. You can't count on the public not noticing the things you miss, or the things you've decided aren't important. They'll notice, and they'll decide every time whether or not they're still going to be your customers tomorrow. Quite often, that answer will be no.

Jason Binn, the publisher of such dynamic publications as *L.A. Confidential, Gotham,* and *The Hamptons,* knows that every detail, no matter how minuscule it may seem, will be spotted by a consumer. "Everything you do is part of a domino effect," Binn says. "When you walk out of your room and you don't put the suit you wore the night before away, or you don't hang up the tie, it won't make any difference—unless someone walks into your room. Then it sends a message that you didn't take pride in your personal hygiene or your living environment."

By the same token, a sloppy corporate appearance can signal to consumers that your business doesn't care about its product, service, or physical plant. That can lead to questions about your commitment to quality, to service, and to serious business practices.

Because I am in the public relations business, I know about image. I know that a business that wants to project a certain image must take every step possible toward making it consistent. There can't be so much as one single detail that doesn't conform to the image the company is trying to project, or it will be found, it will be publicized, and it will be exploited. There is no covering up; there is merely damage control. It's infinitely better, believe me, to have no damage in the first place.

The public doesn't even always know what it wants, but it always knows what it *doesn't* want, and it will not be shy in making that known. The television landscape, for example, is littered with shows that the networks thought couldn't miss, the critics adored, the Emmys honored—and nobody watched. Broken windows? There must have been—if the programming was *that* good and no one watched it, the only explanation lies in broken windows. Perhaps the scheduling was bad, the publicity was ineffective, or the advertising not thought through properly. But something had to go wrong, or *Sports Night* would still be on the air.

The classic example is one of the most famous: the 1980s battle between videotape formats—VHS vs. Sony's Betamax (remember *that?*). Sony had a technology that virtually everyone in the consumer electronics business admitted was better, more efficient, longer lasting, and destined for history. It even had the good sense to make it to the market first, usually a crucial factor in a contest between two closely competing products.

But Beta didn't happen. A difference that many in the industry thought would be a boon for Sony's format—the fact that Beta cassettes were smaller—turned out to be a broken window. VHS, which was developed by JVC and Panasonic's parent company, Matsushita, had wider, larger cassettes, which meant that more tape could fit inside them. Therefore, a VHS cassette, taping at the standard speed, could store up to two hours of programming, whereas a Beta cassette could store only ninety minutes. Industry experts hadn't expected the difference to be important to consumers, but it was a huge broken window that left the format in the dust.

Consumers bought VHS units because they could tape a two-hour movie on one cassette, and Beta—which most believed delivered a better, clearer picture—was finished in a few years. Try to find someone with a Betamax tape deck today. Try to find someone who doesn't still own a VHS machine and a library of tapes. Even with recordable DVD on the market, VHS remains the format of record.

The public saw the broken window and determined that Sony was interested in making a fine product, but not one that did what consumers wanted it to do. When a company loses sight of its customers' needs and wants, and instead concentrates on what it thinks its customers *should* need or want, the company is a giant broken window waiting to happen. Get out of the way before some glass falls on you.

In 1989, the Fox Network was a fledgling group of television stations that didn't broadcast most nights of the week, didn't cover the whole country, and wasn't considered much of a threat to the Big Three—CBS, ABC, and NBC. It was, in fact, considered something of a joke in Hollywood. The Fox Network? A network that didn't even have initials? Please.

That year, programmers at Fox decided to take a very large risk and order a series that was never expected to do very well. An animated sitcom for adults, the show wouldn't offer the kind of heartwarming reassurance that something like *The Cosby Show,* which was the powerhouse of television, did, and it wasn't about to offer real-life situations with flesh-and-blood characters. Besides, cartoons were, um, for kids, weren't they?

There was very little attention paid when the show debuted in 1989, and even as it began to gain momentum, there was confusion in Hollywood. If this was going to be a hit, the conventional wisdom went, how could anything in show business ever make sense again?

Yet *The Simpsons* became more than a hit; it became a genuine, undisputed cultural phenomenon and is considered by a pretty large group to be among the best comedies ever offered on television. And, oh yeah, it became something of a billion-dollar franchise for Fox, launched the network into the stratosphere, and is now in its sixteenth season, the longest for any television comedy in history.

The following year, a powerhouse producer of television drama decided he could take the genre and do something completely unexpected with it. Steven Bochco had produced such fare as *Hill Street Blues* and had almost single-handedly reinvented the police show, and in 1990, everything he did was considered magic.

Then came *Cop Rock*, a show in which the police officers would take time out to illustrate their emotions in song. Big-name songwriters like Randy Newman were commissioned to create original tunes for the show. This was going to be an innovation like nothing before.

It didn't last a whole season.

The public was willing to watch unconventional shows and was that very year embracing *The Simpsons* and turning its characters into cultural icons. The singing cops on *Cop Rock* are considered a blip on the TV radar.

Was *Cop Rock* a broken window? From a business standpoint, not really. The network that took a chance on the show knew it had something extremely unconventional on its hands and didn't hide that fact. The executives who gave the show a green light were counting on the innovative producer who had come through so brilliantly before. It just didn't work.

The broken window came in the process. Somewhere in the midst of the development of the program, through reading the scripts, seeing the pilot episode, discussing the story lines, and (I'm confident) screening what was on film for focus groups of television watchers, didn't it ever occur to anyone that this was *too* innovative, *too* different? Apparently not, or at least no one was willing to say out loud that in this case, the emperor wasn't wearing any clothes. Or that the emperor couldn't carry a tune.

You can't tell the public what it wants. You can only find out, *from* the public, what it *doesn't* want.

The key is to keep an eye, and an ear, open to the consumer at all times. That doesn't just mean you should have customer service representatives available to answer questions and assist with problems at all times. It means you have to constantly seek out consumers, ask your own questions, and *listen to the answers,* whether they're the ones you want or not. Ego is a broken plate-glass window; it's huge, and it overshadows all else. If you want to hear only nice things about yourself, don't ask anyone except your mother.

Don't wait to hear about broken windows from employees or consumers. If you're hearing from a consumer, you can assume that a thousand more noticed the problem and didn't mention it, and you've lost a hefty percentage of those as your customers for life, or at least quite a long time (consumers don't forgive easily, but they do sometimes forgive). If you're finding out about the problem from an employee, you risk losing some respect, since the employees know you should have spotted it first. Do your own dirty work and walk the floor of your retail outlets. Call the office and see how many rings it takes for someone to pick up the phone. Ask for customer service and present the representative with a problem. Pretend it's not your business, but another one with which you have a genuine problem, and see it through less biased eyes. Are things running as smoothly as they should be?

I didn't think so.

GIVE THE PEOPLE WHAT THEY WANT

- Never assume that your consumers "won't notice" broken windows. You might as well close the business today.

- Assume that one disgruntled consumer has friends. And they will hear about how your business's broken windows affected that consumer's experience. The ripple effect could be disastrous.

- Image is important, and a broken image is a broken window. Always have your business's image in mind, even when you're not dealing directly with the public.

- Having a superior product doesn't guarantee success. Having superior customer service and fixing broken windows almost always do.

Chapter Fourteen

The Ultimate Broken Window

If a customer in your bookstore notices that the wallpaper is a little faded, that's a broken window. But it's a broken window that is easily repaired: you can replace the wallpaper with a minimum of difficulty and an affordable expense (in most cases).

What's more important is that the customer in a bookstore probably won't stop coming to the store because the wallpaper is faded. Yes, her image of the company might be a bit diminished, and she might indeed wonder if the books are dusted often enough, but if the titles that customer wants are in stock and the prices are acceptable to her, she will likely overlook the wallpaper unless and until another broken window makes itself known to her.

That will not be true if the broken window occurs in customer service.

I know, you've read it here before, but this point can't possibly be stressed vehemently enough: *Bad customer service is the ultimate broken window.* There is nothing more damaging to your business than the consumer's belief that you don't care about what is bothering him or her.

Think about it: You offer a product or service to the public or a segment of the public. Every member of that group has a right to expect that you will deliver that service or product to their satisfaction. It's not an option; it's a necessity, in order to have anything even resembling a successful business.

In the case of customer service, we have the person who is meant to provide that service or product interacting directly with the public. This is the person who is the face of your business to the consumer. And if that encounter goes badly, especially because the person entrusted with delivering service doesn't do so, it goes beyond worn carpets and loose neckties. It enters into the realm of deal breaker.

It doesn't take a huge amount of imagination to understand that a person who enters a business expecting something—anything—and not getting it will be disappointed. Take that idea a little further, and you'll see that one bad customer service experience—one—can take a customer and turn him or her into a former customer in a heartbeat. No second chances.

Think about this disturbing scenario: You go to a restaurant and order spaghetti; when your order comes, you find an insect crawling on your pasta. Here's my question: Are you going to throw out the bug and eat the spaghetti, or are you going to insist that the entire plate be removed?

Or will you leave the restaurant? And even when that is done, how likely are you to go to that restaurant again?

Exactly.

Customer service isn't just the department where complaints are addressed. It's any encounter between an employee of your company (or, if we extend this idea as far as it goes, any representative of your company, including your product) and the people who might ever be interested in buying your product or service. Any encounter. Sales personnel are involved, clearly, in customer service—they serve the customer directly. But those who deliver the product, service it, and install it are also involved in customer service. The receptionist who answers the phone is a customer service employee. The people who drive your trucks, write your press releases, design your packaging, and pay your bills are all customer service employees. *You* are a customer service employee.

This means you can't afford to have any employee of your organization have a negative encounter with a consumer (and we should make it clear that every business has consumers, not just the ones that sell a product directly to the public). Each person in your employ is an ambassador representing your company in its relations with other nations, and every human being on this planet is another nation, by our definition.

A good ambassador keeps in mind that the art of diplomacy is his first and best tool. Are some customers going to be unreasonable? Of course, some will. Does that mean an employee is justified in treating that person in a curt or irritated manner? Absolutely not.

Every business deals with disgruntled customers, even those that work business-to-business. And in many cases, those customers will not understand the workings of your business and will therefore demand something that you really and truly can't deliver. Many of these will be belligerent or unreasonable and will not approach your employee in a friendly, jovial, accepting manner.

These are the very people to whom your employees must be most accommodating. An ambassador knows that the loudest, nastiest, least reasonable representative of another country is the one who can cause him the most trouble. That belligerent diplomat will go back to his capital, report that although he was making a most understandable demand, it was met with total ambivalence or, worse, outright contempt, and he will recommend that diplomatic relations with the other country be discontinued immediately.

By the same token, a loud and unreasonable customer does not see herself that way. She sincerely believes that her complaint is justified and natural, that her needs, indeed, demand action, and fast action at that. She thinks that your employee, in denying her request, is the one being rigid and unhelpful.

Furthermore, trying to dissuade a customer from complaining is counterproductive. The customer should be made to believe that the company agrees that her complaint is justified and is doing everything it can to correct the problem. Thanking the complainer for pointing out the broken window (real or imagined, in your estimation) is not a bad tactic. Think of the times that you have brought a problem to the attention of a company you have dealt with, as a colleague or a consumer. Which would you have preferred: being told you were wrong in your complaint or being appreciated for your observation and told specifically what would be done to rectify the problem?

Every relationship has a seller and a buyer. Yes, every relationship. And this means that in every situation, someone wants something from the other, and someone is deciding whether or not to grant that request. In business, the lines are usually very well drawn, and we know very clearly who is selling and who is buying. But when problems arise and one of the parties decides a complaint must be made, everything changes.

Keep in mind that a customer who is voicing a complaint is already in a state of mind you'd rather avoid. This person is likely to be irritated and could very well be agitated to the point of behavior that is not characteristic of the relationship as it has been established to this point. Voices might be raised. Unfamiliar words (or at least those that have not been used in the relationship up to this point) might be uttered.

The key is not to respond in kind. *Two* angry people are going to get a lot less done than one angry person and one who is keeping a cool head. You can make points with all your customers by making sure you remain calm and collected in all dealings, especially when they don't do the same. It demonstrates control and reiterates the point that you are taking the situation seriously and trying everything you can to help resolve it to their satisfaction.

All of your employees need to have this idea drummed into their heads on a regular basis. It doesn't matter how agitated and verbally abusive a customer might get, there is no excuse for returning that attitude in kind, and any employee who does so will be fired on the spot, no matter how justified the abrasive behavior may seem at the time.

No exceptions, no second chances, no excuses. Fired. On the spot.

Poor customer service is the ultimate broken window because customer service is the one thing that every business must deliver to its consumers. A breach of that trust, an employee whose actions indicate that he or she is not interested in the customer's concerns, is as blatant and damaging a broken window as you can imagine. And a muddled chain of command is as bad as an obnoxious employee.

I hope you've never had to spend any time in a hospital, but if you have, you probably understand the idea of poor customer service. Members of the support staff (that is, anyone except doctors) in a hospital know their jobs extremely well, I'm sure. They understand the routine, speak the language of medicine, and know the reasons that things work the way they do for patients.

The problem is, the patient is not included in this particular information stream. Patients are generally worried about their health and might not be reacting to situations the way they normally react to stress when living their normal lives. They are, understandably, on edge. But patients also don't understand the routine of hospital work: the time at which certain things are done, the jargon that surrounds virtually any aspect of health care, the reasons that doctors appear when they appear and leave the orders that they leave. Patients don't live in the hospital for a good chunk of their lives, and so they don't "get" the rules the way staff members, who have had years of experience, do.

So when patients are told that things are the way they are and that they, the patients, must adhere to rules they don't understand and have never encountered before, they are likely to be a little less calm and pleasant than they might in another situation.

The problem is, I've yet to find a hospital where the staff understands this. Indeed, they seem to think that patients *should* know what they, the trained staff, know and that patients are simply being obtuse—or worse, stupid—when they ask questions or challenge a rule that to the staff is perfectly justified. There is less explaining and more complaining in hospitals than anywhere else on the planet, in my experience.

Dr. Robert Kotler, a prominent Beverly Hills plastic surgeon, says his practice is run with the idea that the patient should be included in every aspect of care, and he makes it a top priority to hire support staff (nurses, receptionist, office manager and so on) who will empathize and understand a patient's needs.

"Before they get to see the doctor, patients deal with the office staff on the phone, in the office, and in the examining room," he says. "If they have an experience that is unpleasant with one of those people, they'll have a bad taste in their mouth before I walk into the room, and I might not be able to change that. It won't matter how well I do my job if the people who run the office can't validate the valet parking ticket. The patient will already have a bad impression of my practice."

Customer service relates to every aspect of business, and once it becomes a broken window, it is remarkably hard to repair. Remember the insect in the spaghetti? No matter how apologetic the restaurant owner might be, and how diligently he might ensure that the situation can never recur, how likely do you think it is that the customer will return for another chance?

Now, it's possible that you might gain more customers after the changes are implemented to increase customer satisfaction, but how many have you lost for life before that happens? Find out what your customers' concerns are by mystery shopping yourself and asking the most disgruntled of your customers to mystery shop your business for you (turn an enemy into an ally) and give them some discount or free incentive to do so. Yes, you can do it yourself, and you should, but only in addition to the people who are going to be most critical and who don't have the emotional attachment you have to your business and the people in it.

Poor customer service is the ultimate broken window. Excellent customer service is the ultimate pristine, clear, clean window. Which would you rather have?

CAN I HELP YOU?

- A product failure or glitch in delivery creates bad will. Bad customer service loses you a customer for life.

- *All* employees are customer service employees. Everyone in the company does something that affects the consumer's experience with the company. Doing so without respect for the consumer is fatal.

- Each employee is an ambassador for the company, in all dealings with other people. If the employee talks to a friend about the company, the employee is representing the company. Employees must know they are important "faces of the company" and must act accordingly.

• Support staff matters. If you think an employee who doesn't provide the core service of the company isn't representing the company in all dealings with the public, you are asking for trouble.

Chapter Fifteen

What a Difference a Pianist Makes

What is the opposite of a broken window?

Throughout this book, I've been discussing the idea of avoiding and repairing the little things that can go wrong and make a business seem uncaring, incompetent, or simply bad. And we've also looked at the idea of going "above and beyond the call" of customer service, to do more than is expected and to exceed a reasonable expectation on the part of the customer. We've examined businesses that have done well and repaired their broken windows quickly and efficiently.

But what about something that goes beyond? What about a business that goes out of its way to improve the level of customer service in its industry? What about businesses that do things that aren't just unexpected but unprecedented? If you break new ground and raise the level of discussion into something that's never been considered, let alone accomplished, before, is that fixing a broken window, or is it something . . . more?

On the surface, Nordstrom is a department store much like other department stores. Its locations, in shopping malls or stand-alones around the country, offer roughly the same merchandise as, say, Macy's, Bloomingdale's, or Lord & Taylor. Its salespeople are instructed to be helpful, and they do offer more services than most, but they are not so efficient as to be considered a new standard for service in the industry. Its prices are usually competitive with its closest rivals, and occasionally better, when on sale, but sometimes higher than others, too. It's not the discount pricing that's bringing shoppers into Nordstrom, trust me.

So, what, then? If you can buy the same article of clothing at another department store, and one store is not a lot farther from your home than the other, and the pricing is competitive but not demonstrably better, what brings a shopper into Nordstrom and not another store that would be just as easy to patronize?

Am I crazy, or is it the pianist?

In the common area of many Nordstrom locations, where virtually every shopper in the area can see and hear, the company has taken some prime floor space where more upscale merchandise might be displayed, and instead installed a grand piano, and a pianist is most often sitting at it, playing beautifully. The music can be heard throughout the area but is not loud or intrusive. It is undeniably live.

It's not easy to measure, or even to describe, the effect that this live music has on the shopping experience. Customers actually smile as they walk through the area. Some stop to listen for a while. They applaud at the end of a song, and the well-dressed musician acknowledges the appreciation, then moves on to the next piece.

There is no tip jar on the piano. That's important. Very important. This is not the store asking for more of your money, and it's not a way for the pianist to bring in extra bucks.

So you see that the absence of a tip jar on the piano at Nordstrom is especially significant. It represents the store's attempt to provide something extra—and to expect nothing more for the effort.

In fact, it could be argued by efficiency experts that the inclusion of the piano in a department store is a negative thing. It takes up a good deal of floor space that, as I noted, might be used to sell more merchandise. It requires not only an expensive musical instrument that must be purchased and maintained but also an experienced and talented musician to play it. It requires in fact a number of talented musicians, since one couldn't possibly be there to play every hour the store is open every day of the week.

And, as I also noted above, it does not bring a single dime into the store, even for the musician's benefit.

Now, that's the very definition of an added benefit. Here's a corporation thinking about its customers in a way that most don't. It asks nothing and provides a signature touch that will enhance the consumer's experience in the store without diminishing at all from the core business—selling clothing and other merchandise.

If that's not the polar opposite of a broken window, I have no idea what is.

This is not the only example of such a thing in business, by a long shot. But the Nordstrom piano might indeed be the most obvious, the most successful, and the most perfect *unbroken* window in business. It's noticeable—and indeed, became a defining feature of the store; if you say "Nordstrom piano," many people know what you mean—and it speaks volumes about the dedication and thought that goes into Nordstrom's business practices. Does that mean Nordstrom is the best department store chain in the country? Not necessarily. You might feel better about shopping at Macy's or Bloomingdale's (or for that matter, at Target or Wal-Mart), but you can't say you didn't know that Nordstrom has a pianist playing during shopping hours. And you can't say that it doesn't conjure up an image that other department store chains simply don't attempt.

In adding a touch of luxury to an experience that's usually fraught with stressful rushing, tedium, and expense, Nordstrom shows itself to be a company that doesn't just fix its broken windows or do its best to avoid breaking new ones; it makes the statement that Nordstrom is trying to find ways to make the experience of shopping more relaxing and enjoyable, not just more acceptable or less unpleasant. That's more than fixing broken windows; it's a declaration of concern for the people who shop in the store, not those who work there or own the chain, and many customers find that sentiment refreshing.

Consider another company, albeit one not as upscale, that tries to anticipate its consumers' needs and to add touches that will make the experience easier and less stressful. Ikea sells furniture that in most cases the consumer will take home in a box and assemble. It is not in the same neighborhood, in terms of its price structure, as upscale furniture boutiques, where designer items are sold with designer price tags attached.

But Ikea understands its consumer base. Most of the people who come to the chain to buy furniture are just starting out and need affordable but sturdy and useful furniture. The clientele tends to be younger and less affluent than in the fancier stores that sell high-end furniture. Many of the consumers at Ikea are families, especially younger families, trying to find the right furniture for a first home or to furnish children's rooms.

Hence the Ball Room.

In a play area for children, loaded with plastic balls in primary colors, parents can drop off their children while at the Ikea location. The children can play in the ball area (it's like a sandbox without the mess, and the kids can dive in and immerse themselves) or watch a video under supervision by adults. The parents, who sign their children in when entering the store, can look for the items they need without any worry about their children—and without the children expressing boredom with the shopping experience.

This not only makes Ikea a much more family-friendly furniture store, it also makes the experience much more pleasant for those of us who don't want to listen to bored children complaining. It is also a brilliant stroke on the part of Ikea, making the experience more pleasant for everyone (including the kids, who have a wonderful time) and making sure that parents can spend more time shopping for more items—and spending more money—with no impatient children asking "Can we go home now?"

Talk about a win-win situation! The store makes out like a bandit, getting more parents (who are famous for sharing information about kid-friendly stores with other parents) to shop for more items, having children anything but upset about having to go shopping, making a better experience for those who come without children, and costing only a relatively small area of the store, on a floor where there really isn't any merchandise on display, and some employees to supervise the children. When the store is really crowded, the Ball Room might set a time limit, and then parents are paged and asked to pick up their children at a certain time. This ensures that everyone who wants to use the Ball Room during their visit to Ikea will be able to do so and have some uninterrupted shopping time. Oh, and by the way, the Ball Room service is completely free of charge. Try finding a babysitter who charges $0 an hour.

Now, given its merchandise type and price structure, Ikea could probably have gotten away without including the Ball Room in its stores. It would probably have established just as strong a reputation, but it would not be the *same* reputation. It would have been thought of among its target audience—young adults and young families—as that place where you can find inexpensive furniture that has interesting Swedish names.

Instead, what Ikea managed to build was a reputation as a place that *understands families and is trying to help.* It didn't have to say that's what it was doing. Ikea created that statement without having to tell anyone about it—it simply demonstrated the concern by anticipating a need and filling it. And it let its consumers tell its story among the uninitiated. The strategy worked perfectly, mostly because it was based on reality. Ikea really did provide a service that hadn't been asked for, and because of that, it communicated a message that words couldn't have done as effectively.

That's good branding, but it's also the definition of a nonbroken window. This wasn't a bad situation that was corrected; it was a *good* situation that was created before anyone realized it was needed. By the time Ikea had established itself in this country and included a Ball Room in each location, it was too late for competing retail chains to catch up without looking like "me-too" followers.

Companies that anticipate, rather than react to, a need will always be a step ahead of the competition; that goes without saying. But when that anticipation is based not only on sales projections and market research but also on a concern for the core consumer of the merchandise or service, the resulting action will be seen as a real service. Consumers will believe, without being told by advertising, that the company cares about their concerns and is doing something to help. That perception is invaluable, but it can't be faked.

It helps if you are a consumer of the type of product or service you sell, or if you have been a consumer of it in the past. If so, you will know what the needs, the concerns, the problems, of your consumer might be, and you might be able to anticipate a need that you can fill before the customer even knows he or she has it.

If you manage to do that, you will have done more than simply fixing a broken window. You will have created a new, clean, sparkling window that no one could see through before, and a glimpse at the lovely view on the other side.

PIANIST ENVY

- Providing more than the customer expects is good. Providing something the customer wants before she knows she wants it is great.

- Prove to your customer that you know her concerns, care about her welfare, and have a plan to help her with something, and you will create a friend (and a customer) for life. That's more than fixing broken windows; it's creating an impression in the consumer's mind that you know her and care about her.

- Gestures don't have to be profit-driven. Assume that if the consumer believes you have her best interests in mind, she will visit your business more often and spend more money there.

Chapter Sixteen

Broken Windows, No Building

It's not always easy to spot the broken windows in any business. Carpet starts wearing the minute after people start walking on it; at what point does it become a broken window? Fifteen of your on-floor sales staff are right on top of their jobs and doing everything possible to help their clients; one is falling down on the job, not adhering to the dress code, coming in looking disheveled, and you know he has short-term problems at home that might be contributing to his decline. When does he become a broken window?

Now imagine that there is no store, no visual cue to notice. You're operating out of an office, in a business that doesn't sell a product or service to the public in retail stores. You're working from home or through the Internet or as a catalog mail-order business. All the usual broken windows are still important, except the ones that pertain to issues of physical plant. No, you don't have to worry about the wallpaper on your walls or the shirt you're wearing. But if you think you don't have to concern yourself with broken windows as much as those who operate out of brick-and-mortar facilities, you are mistaken.

You have to worry about broken windows even more.

Consider this: Businesses working out of physical retail stores have many more sensory inputs to distract their customers from minor broken windows. If the carpet is a little worn, well, perhaps the bright lights, wall displays, and music piped in through the stereo system will make that less noticeable. If there's a spill in aisle 12, it's entirely possible the customer will overlook that in favor of the sign announcing a sale on an item in aisle 8.

But if the customer's entire experience with your company is conducted on the phone, by mail, or on the Internet, or if your service requires that someone from your company visit the customer at his or her home or business, there will be no distractions from impressive signage or a song being pumped into the ear of your client. There will be, simply, the service the customer receives from your staff, and we've already seen that customer service can be a broken window when even the slightest thing goes wrong.

Think about the experiences you've had with businesses you can't physically visit yourself. When you call Lands' End, for example, you are almost guaranteed to have a more satisfying experience than you will if you call Wal-Mart and ask for customer service in their clothing department.

Why? Because Lands' End, until very recently, never sold one item of clothing inside a retail outlet. (The company, a wholly owned subsidiary of Sears, has recently begun selling its merchandise in Sears stores, but it has never opened a retail store in its own name.) It doesn't have rack after rack of merchandise for you to browse, to feel, to try on before you make a purchase. All it has is a catalog, a Web site, and an army of customer service representatives who will be the only people ever to deal with the company's customers one-on-one. They'd better be good at what they're doing, and in this case, they almost always are. Lands' End representatives on the phone are trained to be polite, accommodating, and helpful, and they do so in such a natural and unforced manner that you'd never know they were carefully trained.

You see, it's not enough to *pretend* to be pleasant. Even in a face-to-face encounter with a sales or service staff member, a customer can tell the difference between a real smile and a trained, forced, phony one. The staff (excuse me, cast members) at Disney World are hired for their ability to perform their jobs without showing the seams. The smiles really aren't saccharine there; they are genuine and believable because the hiring practices from the top down make sure the right people are in the right jobs.

On the phone, you can't see the smile, but you can certainly hear the attitude. And when the customer service personnel is, as is too often the case these days, outsourced to a country where English is not the first language spoken, there can be problems with American customers.

10 Ways to Avoid Face-to-Phone (or -Screen) Broken Windows

1. If nothing else, remember this: **Hire only those people whom you can trust to be accommodating, pleasant, and helpful to deal directly with your customers.** They aren't just your first line of defense; they're the *only* representatives you have with the people who pay your bills. Nothing is more important.

2. **Train your customer service employees diligently.** Do not rely on their peers to "show them the ropes," and don't post your priorities in a lovely framed parchment declaration. Talk to employees. Explain why this is the top priority of the company and why they are the frontline representatives who must do better than expected to do as well as they should.

3. **Don't compromise on customer relations.** If a voice is the only thing your customers are hearing, make sure that voice speaks the language most of your customers speak, fluently and understandably. If you have a multilingual clientele, have representatives who speak the languages you need, fluently. And then add a message system prompt that will get the right customers to the right representatives. Heavy accents are not acceptable on the phone.

4. **Arm your troops well.** Make sure they have the information they need at their disposal quickly and easily. Don't make them ask a supervisor every time a customer has a question. Keep them up-to-date on

company policies and product changes. Make sure they have the answers to the questions.

5. **Allow for creative solutions.** Let your customer service representatives help your customers in ways that might not seem standard. Let them find solutions for each problem and keep each customer happy, and reward them for that. Don't tell your employees that they can't think outside the box, or your customers will believe your business to be rigid and unreasonable when problems arise—which is the last thing you want.

6. **Cut down on hold time.** When your business is based on the phone, it is deadly to make customers wait interminably for contact with an actual human. If it's possible for the customer to solve his or her problem via prompts, that's fine, but if he or she needs a human being to discuss the situation, make sure that person is available in only a few minutes, tops. If that means hiring more representatives, it means your business is growing, so do it.

7. **If your business is on the Internet, make sure the links work and that the customer will not get all the way through the purchasing process only to run into a glitch on the last screen**—nothing is more frustrating. Have online personnel available to help on demand.

8. **Ordering by phone or by mail must be simple and easy.** Complicated forms are not over the head of the customer's intelligence, but they might very well be beyond his or her level of patience. Remember that customers are doing you a favor, not the other way around, by purchasing your product. If

you make it hard for them, they might decide against it. A complex form is a broken window.

9. **Mystery shop your people.** Call, log on, send in a form, whatever it is the customer would do—you do it. See what the problems are, how long it takes to complete the process, and how high your level of frustration rises. Those things that aren't working, fix. Those that are demonstrably better than the competition's, reward.

10. **Make sure your employees know that customer service is the most important priority in the business.** Show them by getting your hands dirty and doing some of it yourself every week or every month. Deal with the customers, come up with innovative solutions, find out how difficult it is to retain your equilibrium while someone is screaming through a headpiece that a new toy won't work. Then come up with ways to help the customers and pass them along to the employees.

It's helpful sometimes to consider the origins of a broken window, tracing it back to the source in order to correct it. In most cases, particularly when a business can't rely on in-store personnel, problems begin with unreasonable rules for customer service or with people hired to do that job who aren't qualified by temperament to perform it. In such cases, you have to consider the origin of the rule or the hiring practices that allowed the wrong person on the bus to begin with.

When a rule is made to deal with a customer problem (we don't offer refunds after ninety days, for example) and that rule conflicts with a customer who seems to have a legitimate problem (the product has malfunctioned on the ninety-first day), you have to reconsider the rule. If a set warranty period is not adhered to, the company will be responsible for the product for a lifetime, and some things are not meant to last forever (you'll notice that most things with a "lifetime warranty" are products like a hammer, which would have to go through a serious calamity to malfunction). However, if that rule is strictly followed with no exceptions, there will invariably be customers who will be left frustrated, with a negative view of the company. Is it worth gaining the cost of a replacement product or a repair to lose the customer for life?

Perhaps an accommodation or a compromise can be reached. All right, so the customer whose product stopped working the day after the warranty period ended might not be entitled to a new product. But perhaps he or she can buy another one at a very large discount, or perhaps the company will pay for the shipping if the customer wants to have it repaired. Giving customer service reps leeway to make their own solutions, so long as they don't abuse the privilege and start giving away the company's inventory, is good for the employees and good for your customers, which makes it good for your business.

In the case of a customer service employee who is not suited to such work, the solution is to remove that person from that job and perhaps give him or her a position that doesn't require one-on-one contact with customers. But the root of the problem is your hiring practices. If you're not hiring people with the proper mind-set for a customer service job, is it the employee's fault when he or she can't do that job properly?

Don't just look at a résumé; look at the *person*. If he has the right personality to help customers, he's right for the job, and it doesn't matter if he graduated high school or went to Yale. If he *doesn't* have the right personality to help customers, he's wrong for the job, and it doesn't matter if he graduated high school or went to Yale.

Consider the *root* of the problem, and you can kill the weed. Consider the *solution* to the problem, and you'll be doing a lot of weeding.

OUTSIDE THE BOX

- Businesses that don't have retail locations have to rely on customer service more than others. That means the broken windows are more subtle and much more damaging.

- Let employees think outside the box; let them come up with solutions that satisfy the customer while keeping the company's interest in mind. Applaud efforts to come up with creative solutions; don't insist on such a strict interpretation of the rules that the customer never comes back.

- Broken windows begin at the root. Hire the right people and set the right rules, and there won't be as many broken windows to fix. If you deal only with the immediate situations, today's problem might be solved, but tomorrow's is waiting to blossom.

- Be an example for your employees. Don't expect them to come up with creative solutions and strive to placate customers if you don't do so yourself. They're going to watch you for an example, even when you're not trying to set one. So always try to set one.

- Mystery shop, mystery shop, mystery shop. You can't know what your online, phone-based, or mail-in problems are if you haven't gone through the experience yourself.

Chapter Seventeen

What's in It for . . . You?

When Kelling and Wilson unveiled the broken windows theory in 1982, they knew it would stir up discussion, argument, and controversy in the world of law enforcement, and I expect this book will have a similar effect among people who own businesses or are interested in business generally. It is not "business as usual," and it is not "the way things have always been done." It is meant to unsettle some people, to shake up the status quo, and to motivate business owners and employees into a new way of thinking about the way they go about their work and their lives.

After all, as you've read, the broken windows theory for business is based on the premise that something is wrong—very wrong—with the way most businesses are run in this and other countries. It presumes that most small mistakes, most oversights and neglected details, are not being noticed or, worse, corrected, and that in turn presumes that most business owners are not as invested, intellectually and emotionally, in the businesses they run.

Throwing money at a business and expecting it to perform well is not enough. If the owner and the people who work for him or her are not committed, to the point of exhaustion and obsession, to the work they do, the business will not be as successful as it could be. In most cases, in fact, it will not be successful at all.

It's estimated (and this is apocryphal) that over 70 percent of the restaurants that open in Manhattan will fail within two years. Is it because the owners didn't have a good idea? Because they served bad food? Because people in New York City aren't hungry? It happens because the details—the broken windows—are not being anticipated or repaired and, in many cases, because the restaurant owners don't know what they should be looking for. People simply don't believe that details amount to much. I think in the course of this book, we've seen that they do.

I've told you about the tiny things that have made huge differences, both good and bad. I've mentioned names of companies—some of which probably wish I hadn't—and pointed to examples you'd probably heard about before but hadn't considered in just this way. Now you know that the details make an enormous difference, and you know just how all-encompassing a pursuit it is to run a business successfully, keeping an eye on all the windows for the first signs of cracks.

Throughout this book, you have read about companies that ignored their broken windows or never saw them in the first place. You've also read about companies that not only repaired their broken windows but anticipated them and went above and beyond the call of duty to stay ahead of the curve and give customers more than what they might logically have been expecting.

But what do all those stories mean to *you*? If you're not the owner of a huge fast food chain, a major clothing retailer, or a movie star, what could it possibly matter to you if a company sinks or swims based on its dedication to detail? Why should you care if the coffee is too hot, the carpet is worn, or the counter staff doesn't smile enough (or at all)? Perhaps you own one small dry cleaning outlet or a company that provides information technology services to other businesses. Does it matter to you whether the people serving hamburgers know how to speak English?

It should.

Maybe the examples you've read about in these pages aren't directly related on a physical level to your own. Maybe you don't have counter staff or sell a physical product. But the lessons learned have implications that go far beyond those concrete examples. They are meant to open your mind to the concept of broken windows for business and to build your own bridges to the issues that will make or break the business you've chosen to be in.

The parable about Kmart, for example, was to illustrate the concept of Broken Windows Hubris, one of the deadliest forms of broken windows, in which companies get the idea that they are larger and more powerful than the people who, by way of patronizing them, keep the company in business. Even a small company suffers from this disorder when it decides that it has become popular, that its customers are loyal and therefore complacent, and that the business can run on automatic pilot for a while. That's when the broken windows are guaranteed to shatter, loudly.

It's important to find the concept behind the story and

to extrapolate it to your own situation. That's why the summaries at the end of each chapter have been included: to help you recap what you've read and perhaps to decide on your own how you might apply the concept to your own business.

You know your business much better than I can. You know the particulars of the trade you're in and how they relate to the people you consider your clientele. I can't hope to make that claim for every industry in which a person who reads this book might be employed. But I *can* tell you about the broken windows theory for business, and you can make the leap from there. See if these concepts don't strike a chord with you, as some of them are universal and can be applied to every business:

- **Obsession and compulsion are vital to a manager's mastery of broken windows.** There is no excuse for letting something go when you know it could be improved, and there is no excuse for not caring enough.

- **Employees are vital to every business, whether they have direct contact with the general public or not.** But when employees are given contradictory signals from management (when, for example, a directive to punch in on time every day is posted over the time clock, and then the department manager comes and goes as he or she pleases), the employees will understandably be confused and irritated, and will become broken windows.

- **The worst broken windows may be people.** Employees who have the wrong attitude, who don't care about the company (and, by extension, the customer), will become a virus that will spread throughout the ranks.

Eventually, if these employees are not dealt with noticeably and either corrected or removed, the majority of the company's employees will become infected with the virus and could pass it on to the rest. Swift action is absolutely imperative.

• **Appearance *does* matter.** The physical look of your business, from the walls to the carpet to the windows (broken, dirty, or otherwise) to the employees, is going to make an impact on the image your customers see. This is just as true when your clientele doesn't come to the premises if you present the image of the company through advertising, in company vehicles, or through the representatives you send into the field. Uniforms are an option, since they present a, well, *uniform* image, but in any event, proper appearance is very important. Maintenance on company vehicles and especially on the company premises is extremely noticeable. Especially when it isn't done.

• **When a customer deals with your business, he or she expects something.** Your business has three options at that point: It can meet the expectation, it can exceed the expectation, or it can fail to meet the expectation. Guess which one is best and which is not acceptable. It can be beneficial sometimes to promise *less* than you know you will deliver, in order to best exceed expectations and make a positive reputation for your business.

• It sounds New Agey and silly to discuss a customer's "experience" when dealing with, say, a plumbing company or a business-to-business service company, but when all is said and done, **what the customer experiences in dealing with your business will determine**

whether you will see that customer again. Yes, some of that experience will depend on the quality of the product and the price the customer has to pay, but the variables—the broken or unbroken windows—will make the majority of the difference in most cases. Make the customer's experience a pleasant, even rewarding, one, and you have a much better chance of making a friend for life.

• It can't be stressed enough: **The only way to know what a customer experiences in dealing with your business is to act like a customer yourself.** Walk the floor of the business, call the office and see what that's like, register a complaint (even if you don't have one) and see how your staff handles the situation. Only when you have lived as a customer can you best anticipate the needs of the customer, and that is half the battle in fixing the broken windows. If you're too recognizable to the staff, get someone you know and trust implicitly to do so. Find the customers who register the most complaints and give them an incentive to mystery shop the business and report back to you.

• **In cyberspace, everyone can hear you scream.** Internet broken windows travel faster and spread farther than any other kind. Sometimes they're not controllable, but most of the time they are. Keep a sharp eye on your Web site and make sure six times over that your online customer support representatives and the mechanisms they operate are always working properly.

• **Give the customer *more* than you should, and you will make an impression.** Fix windows that aren't broken by using your experience to think like your customer, and determine what would impress you. Then provide that.

These are just a few of the ways you can apply the broken windows theory for business to your own industry. There are literally millions of ways to do it, but you don't need a list. What you need is what I hope this book has provided for you: a new outlook on business that includes, and in fact stresses, a devotion to detail.

Broken windows can come from any aspect of business, and they can be dealt with if you know what to look for. What's important to take away from the experience of reading this book is the desire to find those cracks: the obsessive, compulsive, almost violent need to find the flaws before they become damage, and to eradicate them as swiftly and completely as possible. It's a never-ending job, and one that requires a ruthless dedication and an insatiable hunger for excellence. No: *Perfection.*

As I noted before, every relationship, in every aspect of life, has a seller and a buyer. In business, the roles are usually very clear. As a seller, you must consider what the buyer wants, what he or she expects, and what will please and displease him or her. You need to provide the service along with the product that will make an impression, and a favorable one, to attach to your business as a whole. Keeping your windows in one piece is a very strong step in that direction. It's all stagecraft, and it's about not letting them see you sweat. It's about covering up the cracks and making them disappear, and about being on a constant, unending search for potential cracks so you can make them disappear before they appear.

We started with the question: When is a dirty bathroom

a broken window? I hope that question has been answered in these pages, more than once. And I hope it has launched ten thousand other questions you've already begun to ask yourself about your own business, about what you can do to improve it, to make it *seem* better, and to make it really and truly better. Because once you've embraced the concept of broken windows, you can't ever go back. It's a curse and a blessing. You'll be left with the power to see the breaks and the determination to fix every last one of them.

It's an awesome concept, and one that you should now just be starting to use on your own. If you do, I promise you, your business will be a more efficient, more impressive, more effective one in a relatively short time. But this is not the kind of idea you can implement a little bit. Fixing and maintaining your broken windows will be an all-encompassing activity, or it will be none at all. You'll find yourself thinking about it when you're lying in bed at night and when you wake up in the morning. Your mind will wander to possible breaks in your business's windows when you're in the shower or having dinner. You'll notice things others will miss, and even when you point them out, I warn you, they will deny such things exist or insist they are unimportant and that you are being ridiculous, obsessive, and paying too much attention to trivial details.

But you and I both know that there is no such thing as too much attention to detail.

At the end of this chapter, you'll find the Broken Windows for Business Pledge. It's a serious statement outlining the tenets of the broken windows for business theory. It's actually a restatement of everything you've learned in this book, and it should be taken very seriously. I hope you'll read it, and sign it when you're finished.

If you live up to the promises in the pledge and make them second nature, you will discover your business—and maybe your life—running more smoothly and efficiently than ever before.

Good luck with your new knowledge and your new power. I believe that if you use it, you will have positive results. But no matter what, I can definitely guarantee one thing: You will never look at a broken window—or an unbroken one—the same way again.

The Broken Windows for Business Pledge

I, _____, having read the concepts of the broken windows for business theory, do hereby pledge to do the following:

- I will pay attention to every detail of my business, especially those that seem insignificant.
- I will correct any broken windows I find in my business, and I will do so immediately, with no hesitation.
- I will screen, hire, train, and supervise my employees to notice and correct broken windows in the least amount of time possible.
- I will treat each customer like the only customer my business has.
- I will be on constant vigil for signs of Broken Windows Hubris and will be sure never to assume my business is invulnerable.
- I will mystery shop my own business to discover broken windows I hadn't noticed before.
- I will make sure every customer who encounters my business is met with courtesy, efficiency, and a smile.
- I will exceed my customers' expectations.
- I will be sure always to make a positive first impression and will assume that every impression is a first impression.
- I will make sure that my online and telephone customer service representatives do everything possible to solve a customer's problem perfectly the first time.
- I will be obsessive and compulsive when it comes to my business.

Signed the _____ day of _____, in the year

_____, by _____.

Mr. Levine is a frequent speaker at corporations and universities. He can be contacted at mlevine@LCOonline.com.

Index